While You Wait

Pertinent Truths and Lessons Learned during Seasons of Waiting

Susan J. Musgrave

ISBN 979-8-88943-711-6 (paperback)
ISBN 979-8-88943-712-3 (digital)

Christian Faith Publishing
832 Park Avenue
Meadville, PA 16335
www.christianfaithpublishing.com

All biblical citations were taken from the New Living Translation of the Holy Bible unless otherwise indicated.

Cover inspired by Susan Musgrave
Cover designed by Yolande Niles-Harley

Printed in the United States of America

Christian education teacher and mentor,
Woodbrook Pentecostal Church
Port of Spain, Trinidad and Tobago

Written as a testimony of God's great love for us and His concern for our journey through life! This book reminds us of the truth of God's words to never leave nor forsake us. Deuteronomy 31:6 says "So be strong and courageous! Do not be afraid and do not panic before them. For the LORD your God will personally go ahead of you. He will neither fail you nor abandon you." He also promises to be with us till the end of the ages. Matthew 28:20 says "Teach these new disciples to obey all the commands I have given you. And be sure of this: I am with you always, even to the end of the age."

As Susan takes us through the various chapters of her life, we see the faithfulness of God. It is a picture of the relationship that He wants with each one of us. We can take Him at His Word as we trust and obey Him.

Thank you, Susan, for sharing your experiences! Your life is a living testimony, and the journey continues.

—Theresa Andrews
Mentee
Port of Spain, Trinidad and Tobago

CONTENTS

Of all the instructions that God has given to mankind for his upkeep and survival, I can see a number of them speaking about "Waiting on God for directions for ones next move." He says to him, "Wait on the LORD: be of good courage, and he shall strengthen thine heart: wait, I say, on the LORD" (Psalm 27:14 KJV). "Wait on the LORD, and keep his way, and he shall exalt thee to inherit the land:" (Psalm 37:34a KJV).

Susan Isidore is a leader at our church fellowship Woodbrook Pentecostal Church. She is quite capable of teaching the Word of God and leading others into a closer relationship with Him. Her association with younger people is very admirable. After graduating from the West Indies School of Theology, the author joined the *Logos Hope* ship.

Susan had the opportunity to travel to different parts of the world as she served on the *Logos Hope* ship. During her travels, she was focused on declaring that Jesus Christ is Lord and King to people from several nations. Susan learned to wait on the Lord in prayer as her faith and trust in Him grew throughout this season of her life. The Logos teams' work not only consisted of the spiritual aspect but also in practical ways such as helping to build houses, churches, and schools as part of their service. In addition, the teams would help young people in making worthwhile decisions in careers while fostering long-lasting friendships.

Susan Isidore has given much of her life to developing an intimate relationship with God. It is out of this relationship that she was inspired to author this book. Throughout this relationship, Susan acquired a wealth of knowledge and revelations from the Lord that can bless you and be life changing. Enjoy reading and feel yourself changed as your mind is renewed.

—Rev. Joycelyn Nelson
Pastor, Woodbrook Pentecostal Church
Port of Spain, Trinidad and Tobago

My inspiration for writing *While You Wait* was borne out of the process of my journey of waiting on God. This period of waiting took over twenty years before I saw the manifestation of some of God's promises and before I fully understood what He wanted me to learn through this process.

Waiting is never easy, especially if you are used to getting things done on your own timetable and with your own efforts. One of the first things I had to do while on my journey of waiting was to surrender my timetable to the Lord. God showed me that He is the one that has my life and timeline in His hands. I had to place total trust in God for the process of waiting to be successful.

Waiting takes time, but it is during this time that growth and intimacy are fostered. It is God's desire that we know Him, and this is clearly stated in the scriptures. John 17:3 states, "And this is the way to have eternal life—to know you, the only true God, and Jesus Christ, the one you sent to earth." I trust that as you read this book, you will be encouraged and challenged to develop greater intimacy with God, especially during your seasons of waiting.

In the year 1998, I had a life-changing experience with God. This occurrence could be likened to Saul's "Damascus Road" experience in the book of Acts chapter 9. After this experience, God started revealing to me His purpose and plans for my life. Before this revelation, I never thought about my life as being one of purpose nor that the God of the universe was interested in its direction. I thought the road map to life was the same normal pattern for everyone—the pattern that says that one should attend school and obtain a good education, followed by a respectable job, and also that one should find a soul mate, get married, have a family, and live happily ever after, just like in the movies.

I know by now you may be wondering what was my life-changing experience. I was in a committed relationship for six and a half years and was engaged to be married. Just six months before the wedding, the relationship had become strained, so I sought God for direction. After one day of praying and fasting, I felt the Lord saying to me, "This man that you are about to marry is not the person I have chosen for you." This was the first time in my life that I had practiced the discipline of fasting; however, I knew this had helped me in being sensitive to what God was saying to me. My time of fasting gave me clarity on exactly what God wanted me to do next. I now had to end the relationship.

Even though the Lord had given me clear directions, the human side of me still wrestled with the decision I made to end the relationship. During this time of brokenness, I felt like my world had fallen apart. I then started having dreams in which God began revealing more of Himself to me, indicating what my next steps should be. The Lord also revealed certain promises for my life's purpose that I held onto. However, I did not realize it was also the beginning of a process of getting to know God more intimately.

CHAPTER 1

The Process

These are the words of the late apostle Bertril Baird: If we fail while going through the process, we may also fail to be transformed by the process. These words were spoken to a group of us who spent a number of years being discipled by the late apostle. From that day onward, I have kept these precious words at the back of my mind because I understood it meant that I had to yield to what God was doing in and through me to get a successful end.

A process can be defined as a series of actions or steps taken to achieve a particular end. The process can either fail or succeed depending on your attitude and submission toward it. If you do not submit and allow your life to be transformed during the process, you may not reach the fullest potential needed to complete your God-given purpose. I have come to learn and appreciate the fact that Father God is more concerned about the process, because during this time, He teaches us a number of things such as faith, patience, and trust. He has also helped me to understand that, though the process may consist of many seasons of waiting, this time fosters growth and true intimacy with Him.

Surrendering

After my life-changing experience, I surrendered my entire heart to Jesus, and He became my Lord and Savior. I then began the process of surrendering my will so that God's will could be fulfilled in my life. One of the first things I had to surrender was the desire to change my job. At that time, I was gainfully employed for three years at a private firm, working as an accounts receivable clerk. After three years, I was just about ready for a change of environment and a new challenge. As I sought the Lord for direction, I felt Him say to me, "This is where I want you to be at this time, and it's My desire to promote you before you leave this job." The process of surrendering continued for five more years before God opened the door for my promotion to accounting cashier. I worked in this position for two years before it was time to finally leave the firm.

I had to wait on God's timing for seven years before the release came for me to close the chapter at this firm. There were many lessons learned during this season of surrendering as I waited on God's timing. It was also a time when the fruit of the Spirit was being developed in my heart, especially in the area of patience. As a result, my faith and trust in God increased. In Galatians 5:22–23 reads, "But the Holy Spirit produces this kind of fruit in our lives: love, joy, peace, patience, kindness, goodness, faithfulness, gentleness, and self-control. There is no law against these things!"

Surrendering of our will is an ongoing process throughout our Christian journey. We are created with free will, and we are egocentric human beings who are always thinking about pleasing ourselves. This is true for every human being—those who lived in the past, those who are presently alive, and those who will be born in the future. Surrendering our will has to begin with our desire to please the Father and to do His will. We can see this being manifested in Jesus's prayer in the garden of Gethsemane found in Luke 22:42: "Father, if you are willing, please take this cup of suffering away from me. Yet I want your will to be done, not mine."

Jesus wanted His Father to remove "this cup of suffering" from Him. This suffering Jesus faced represented the sin of the world and the separation from His Father. However, Jesus understood that His father needed Him to make this sacrifice to redeem mankind. Jesus desired to do the will of the Father instead of having His own way.

There are times in our lives when the Father will require us to make sacrifices and do certain things that we may not necessarily like or desire. But if we love the Father and desire to please Him, then we will forego our will so that His will could be done in our lives.

There were a few occasions on my journey where I had to use Jesus's words in my prayer. These words helped me to surrender my will to God while desiring His will in my life. During one of the difficult periods, I could remember my lips repeating the scripture that says, "Father, if you are willing, please take this cup of suffering away from me. Yet I want your will to be done, not mine" (Luke 22: 42). However, deep in my heart and spirit, I was crying and saying, "I don't want to do what You are asking me to do." Nevertheless, as the days went by and I continued to pray using Jesus's words, my heart and spirit started to yield. Eventually, I surrendered my will and accepted the will of the Father. God is a loving Father, and He allows the Holy Spirit to help us surrender our will to do His will. This all happens so that the God-given purpose in our lives can be fulfilled.

Learning to Hear God's Voice

My journey with God continued, and so too was the process of learning to hear His voice. God directed me to enroll at the West Indies School of Theology (WIST), where I firstly pursued a diploma and then a degree in Bible and theology. As I read the notices on the board in the foyer area of the Woodbrook Pentecostal Church (WPC), there was a brochure advertising the courses at WIST. I sensed God speaking to me through His Spirit by a thought, *Apply for enrollment at the Bible school.* I was totally surprised by the idea, but I got excited about the thought of learning more about the Bible. I had already developed a great love and passion for the Word of God.

During my time at WIST, as I was learning to hear God's voice, my faith was put into action even more. By faith, I was also putting into practice what was being taught in my Bible courses. "But without faith it is impossible to please Him; for he that cometh to God must believe that he is, and that he is a rewarder of them that diligently seek him" (Hebrews 11:6 KJV).

The time spent at Bible school was years of sacrifice because I had to pay the cost of my tuition. However, I saw God's faithfulness in ordering my steps each semester, whereby enabling me to pay my bills.

I could remember one semester when my faith increased as I obeyed the voice of God. It was my plan to take a small loan from my employer to pay my school fees for the upcoming semester. On the Sunday night of the week in which my school fees were due, I felt the Holy Spirit saying to me, "Do not take the loan, and trust Me to pay your school fees for this semester." The battle went on in my mind for a while, but then I decided to surrender my will and said, "Okay, Father God, I will not take the loan." I then started thinking about the embarrassment I would have to face having to apologize to the accounts clerk for not being able to pay my school fees on time. Nevertheless, I signed up for my courses and graciously asked for some extra time to pay my fees.

God was faithful in keeping His end of the deal. On the following Thursday, my pastor, the late apostle Turnel Joshua Nelson, was the guest speaker at our chapel service. I was not aware of this until I met him at the administration building of the Bible school. After our initial greetings, he asked me, "Have you already paid your school fees?"

My response to him was, "No, I haven't."

He then asked me to give the details of my school fees to the administrator at the WPC church's office so my fees could be paid. I was totally elated by what God had done for me this semester. This further increased my faith and trust in God when I sensed He was speaking to me through His Holy Spirit.

During my years of waiting, as I grew in my relationship with God, so did my sensitivity to hearing His voice as is stated in the book of John, "My sheep hear my voice, and I know them, and they follow me" (John 10:27 KJV).

The Lord also guided me to some of the principles relating to hearing His voice, and I would like to share them with you:

a. *Firstly, we need to develop a God consciousness.*
    In *Psalm 139:1–10,*

> O Lord, you have examined my heart
> and know everything about me. You know

when I sit down or stand up. You know my thoughts even when I'm far away. You see me when I travel and when I rest at home. You know everything I do. You know what I am going to say even before I say it, LORD. You go before me and follow me. You place your hand of blessing on my head. Such knowledge is too wonderful for me, too great for me to understand! I can never escape from your Spirit! I can never get away from your presence! If I go up to heaven, you are there; if I go down to the grave, you are there. If I ride the wings of the morning, if I dwell by the farthest oceans, even there your hand will guide me, and your strength will support me.

b. *Secondly, we need to accept/acknowledge the Holy Spirit as a person.*
    In *John 16:5–15,*

But now I am going away to the one who sent me, and not one of you is asking where I am going. Instead, you grieve because of what I've told you. But in fact, it is best for you that I go away, because if I don't, the Advocate won't come. If I do go away, then I will send him to you. And when he comes, he will convict the world of its sin, and of God's righteousness, and of the coming judgment. The world's sin is that it refuses to believe in me. Righteousness is available because I go to the Father, and you will see me no more. Judgment will come because the ruler of this world has already been judged. There is so much more I want to tell you, but you can't bear it now. When the Spirit of truth comes, he will guide you into all truth. He will not speak on his own but will tell you what he has heard. He will tell you about the future. He will bring me glory by telling you whatever he receives from me. All that belongs to the Father is mine; this is why I said, "The Spirit will tell you whatever he receives from me."

c.   *Thirdly, we need to cultivate or practice knowing the presence of God.*
In *Joshua 1:7–9,*

> Be strong and very courageous. Be careful to obey all the instructions Moses gave you. Do not deviate from them, turning either to the right or to the left. Then you will be successful in everything you do. Study this Book of Instruction continually. Meditate on it day and night so you will be sure to obey everything written in it. Only then will you prosper and succeed in all you do. This is my command—be strong and courageous! Do not be afraid or discouraged. For the LORD your God is with you wherever you go.

In *Proverbs 3:1–7,*

> My child, never forget the things I have taught you. Store my commands in your heart. If you do this, you will live many years,

and your life will be satisfying. Never let loyalty and kindness leave you! Tie them around your neck as a reminder. Write them deep within your heart. Then you will find favor with both God and people, and you will earn a good reputation. Trust in the LORD with all your heart; do not depend on your own understanding. Seek his will in all you do, and he will show you which path to take. Don't be impressed with your own wisdom. Instead, fear the LORD and turn away from evil.

In *John 14:15–21,*

If you love me, obey my commandments. And I will ask the Father, and he will give you another Advocate, who will never leave you. He is the Holy Spirit, who leads into all truth. The world cannot receive him, because it isn't looking for him and doesn't recognize him. But you know him, because he lives with you now and later will be in you. No, I will not abandon you as orphans—I will come to you. Soon the world will no longer see me, but you will see me. Since I live, you also will live. When I am raised to life again, you will know that I am in my Father, and you are in me, and I am in you. Those who accept my commandments and obey them are the ones who love me. And because they love me, my Father will love them. And I will love them and reveal myself to each of them.

God is omnipresent. He is present everywhere. He is omnipotent. This term relates to Him being all-powerful. He is also omniscient. This speaks to the fact that He knows all things. God sees and knows everything about us, so we cannot hide from Him. The sooner we come to terms with this fact, the sooner we will have the consciousness that there is no barrier between us and God. This could be likened to walking under an open heaven where God is seeing us through and through. These truths should also encourage us to live a transparent life before God.

We also need to respect the Holy Spirit as a person and invite Him into our space, which can refer to our daily activities. The Holy Spirit is not a "spooky being" out there in the cosmos, but He is a gentle person with emotions. He is referred to as the third person in the Trinity. The Trinity or Godhead consists of God the Father; God the Son, Jesus Christ; and God the Holy Spirit. The Holy Spirit will not force Himself on anyone, nor will He force anyone to do anything that they do not want to willingly do. Instead, He will gently wait for persons to cooperate with Him as He helps them to walk in obedience to God's will.

Some people may have challenges in accepting the truth about the Trinity. However, this is one of the mysteries in Christianity that we must accept by faith while enjoying the benefits of our beliefs. Father God sent His Son, Jesus Christ, to die for our sins, and Jesus is the only one Who has seen the Father. Just before Jesus left the earth, He said that He would send the Holy Spirit Who is the spirit of truth. Part of His work is to lead, guide, and direct us into all truth. Jesus is the mediator who will go to the Father on our behalf, and the Holy Spirit will reveal to us what Jesus has received from the Father. This is just a simple explanation of the working of the Trinity, and I hope that it has helped to give you some clarity.

In the book of John chapter 16, we can read the words of Jesus which give further understanding of the working of the Holy Spirit.

In *John 16:5–15,*

> But now I am going away to the one who sent me, and not one of you is asking where I am going. Instead, you grieve because of what I've told you. But in fact, it is best for you that I go away, because if I don't, the Advocate won't come. If I do go away, then I will send him to you. And when he comes, he will convict the world of its sin, and of God's righteousness, and of the coming judgment. The world's sin is that it refuses to believe in me. Righteousness is available because I go to the Father, and you will see me no more. Judgment will come because the ruler of this world has already been judged. There is so much more I want to tell you, but you can't bear it now. When the Spirit of truth comes, he will guide you into all truth. He will not speak on his own but will tell you what he has heard. He will tell you about the future. He will bring me glory by telling you whatever he receives from me. All that belongs to the Father is mine; this is why I said, "The Spirit will tell you whatever he receives from me."

For us to become more aware of the presence of God in our daily activities, it is necessary for us to identify the functions of the three persons in the Trinity. God is our Heavenly Father who created everything and is in control of everything in the seen and unseen realms. Jesus Christ is the Savior of the world, and we are saved by grace through faith in Him. Jesus is currently seated at the right hand of the Father, and He is making intercession for the believers in the world. The Holy Spirit is the one Who is currently living in and among us on earth, and He ushers us into the presence of God. The Holy Spirit is given to help us live a successful Christian life. Hence, the reason it is imperative for us to cooperate with Him is so that He could lead, guide, and direct us in all areas of our lives. The Holy Spirit speaks to us through our spirit and uses the Word of God to convict, correct, or rebuke us when necessary.

We would direct our prayers to the Father while praying in the name of the Son Jesus Christ. The Holy Spirit would be the one guiding us on how to pray and what to pray for. The more disciplined we become in studying and meditating on the Word of God, the more we would get to understand the heart of the Father and see the workings of Jesus while experiencing the power of the Holy Spirit in our lives. The more we acknowledge our total dependency on the Holy Spirit, the more He would show up and work on our behalf. This would create the atmosphere for a greater level of intimacy not only with the Holy Spirit but also with the Father and the Son as we practice knowing the presence of God.

Walking in Total Obedience to God's Word

The process of knowing God intimately not only consists of surrendering our will and learning to hear His voice, but it also requires us to walk in total obedience to His Word. This process will take time, and it's a lifelong journey of getting to know the limitless Almighty God. No one will ever get to the place of knowing God entirely, but the more we yield ourselves to Him, the more He will reveal Himself to us.

The Scripture tells us that God is light, and in Him, there is no darkness. Light represents what is good, pure, true, holy, and reliable while darkness represents what is sinful and evil. We are currently living in a dark world because of sin and disobedience. When we obey God by practicing what is written in His Word, the light of the Lord would be emanated from us.

I would often tell people that they would not usually see the devil walking down the street with a pitchfork in his hands, nor would they see God flying around with angelic wings. However, people will see the manifestation of the devil in the world through individuals who are walking in darkness and practicing evil. On the other hand, the manifestation of God will be seen through individuals who are living in the light and practicing what is written in the Word of God.

In *1 John 1:5–10,*

> This is the message we heard from Jesus and now declare to you: God is light, and there is no darkness in him at all. So we are lying if we say we have fellowship with God but go on living in spiritual darkness; we are not practicing the truth. But if we are living in the light, as God is in the light, then we have fellowship with each other, and the blood of Jesus, his Son, cleanses us from all sin. If we claim we have no sin, we are only fooling ourselves and not living in the truth. But if we confess our sins to him, he is faithful and just to forgive us our sins and to cleanse us from all wickedness. If we claim we have not sinned, we are calling God a liar and showing that his word has no place in our hearts.

CHAPTER 2

Commencement of Missionary Journey

One of the convictions that I received from Father God at my conversion was that my life would extend beyond the shores of Trinidad and Tobago. At that time, I did not fully understand what all of this meant, nor was I certain about what the outcome would be. As my Christian journey continued, so too did my knowledge about missions, including the life and work of missionaries. In addition to pursuing several mission courses of study at Bible school, I also began contributing financially (sowing) to the work of missions. I felt God was leading me into the area of sowing in preparation for the future. The Lord knew that, in time, I would need the financial support of others.

I always liked the idea of traveling and meeting people. At one time during my childhood, I had a passing thought about working at the airport so that I could meet people from different countries. Little did I know, God had a plan for my life that would entail traveling and meeting people from different countries and cultures.

After having nurtured the seed for missions in my heart for seven years, my missionary journey began in the year 2005. In July 2005, the Lord directed me to resign from my job of ten years. This major decision was the beginning of learning to "step out on the water" and walk by faith while trusting God. "Then Peter called to him, 'Lord, if it's really you, tell me to come to you, walking on the water.' 'Yes, come,' Jesus said. So, Peter went over the side of the boat and walked on the water toward Jesus" (Mathew 14:28–29).

Two days after leaving the security and comforts of a full-time job, I boarded a plane on a mission trip to Las Amazonas, Venezuela. The mission trip was organized by a team of persons from the Global Missions Centre (GMC) headed by Rev. Don Hamilton. I had been away from my home church for several months because of my internship program at Bible school. It was nearing the end of my studies when I decided to visit GMC before returning to my home church. The Sunday morning when I decided to visit GMC, the rain was falling very heavily. However, I did not want to defer my plans, so I whispered a short prayer for the rain to stop. Thankfully, after a short while, my prayer was answered, and the rain ceased.

During the service at GMC, there was a presentation about an upcoming mission trip. There was a request for pledges toward financial support and also for persons who would be interested in joining the mission team. Immediately, I felt in my Spirit that this would be a good opportunity to experience missions and visit Venezuela. The thought of practicing my Spanish was very exciting. I fell in love with the Spanish language when I was introduced to it during my high school years.

After graduating from high school, I enrolled at the Venezuelan embassy where I continued my studies for a number of months.

I pledged one hundred dollars and said to Father God, "If You want me to go on this trip, then You will have to give me confirmation and also provide the finances." A few weeks after paying my pledge, one of my good friends informed me that she had received some outstanding remuneration and wanted to bless me with one thousand dollars. This monetary gift was given to me by my friend toward a vacation in commemoration of the completion of my studies. However, after thanking my friend for this kind gesture, I immediately said to her, "This money is not to take me on a vacation, but it will go toward the upcoming mission trip to Venezuela." I took this monetary gift as a sign of confirmation from God about going on the mission trip. I also saw this as a blessing because I honored my one-hundred-dollar pledge toward the trip.

The team spent a total of eight days in Venezuela, working in the rural areas of Las Amazonas. During the daytime, some of the team members were involved in constructing a church building while others were involved with children's programs and evangelistic outreach. I thoroughly enjoyed my first mission trip, especially the team dynamics where everyone found their place and served with commitment and diligence. I also got the opportunity to practice my Spanish-speaking skills. I appreciated being immersed in the culture and language of the Venezuelans. I guess it's because of my Spanish heritage from my roots in Paramin, Trinidad. However, I am still working on becoming fluent in the language as it is one of my personal goals.

My second missionary stint was in March 2009 while completing my bachelor's degree at Bible school. There was an introductory class to missions where we did a local mission trip. I was chosen to be the mission coordinator for this class project. This mission's trip lasted three days. The location was at Carapal, Los Iros, which is in the southern part of Trinidad. From the initial planning stages straight through to the end of the trip, the presence of the Lord was sensed by everyone. We saw this not only as a class project but also as God's business, and it was treated with the same efficiency and excellence as if it were a foreign trip.

On this trip, I had one of my mountaintop experiences with Father God, Who chose to use me prophetically during the Sunday morning service. Once again, I realized He was confirming the missionary call on my life. The entire team of thirty persons along with our dear lecturer, Dr. Esther Baisden, stood in awe of God's awesome power and presence evident on that trip. The pastor and his family were tremendously blessed by our visit.

One of the major highlights for everyone was that several people committed their lives to Jesus Christ. One of the persons who gave their life to Christ on that day was the pastor's father. He usually supported his son with work around the church building but had not surrendered his heart to Christ until that day. The manifestation of God's power was very evident.

Around this time, I also got invited to be a part of another mission trip to Grenada in December. My response to the individual was, "If this is God's will for me, then He will confirm it." On another occasion, a second person from the Exodus Mission team asked me to accompany them on the trip. I took note of this, but I still said to God, "If this is You, confirm it."

As time went by, I had a dream in which I received a dollar note with the name Grenada printed on it. One of the ways in which God speaks to me is through dreams. Because of this, I felt settled in my heart that God was saying it is okay to go on this mission trip. As if this was not enough confirmation, in September, my mother jokingly asked me if I wanted a party for my birthday. I told her, "I don't want a party, but it would be nice to send me on a trip." My mother then suggested that I go to Grenada. I just smiled and pondered her response in my heart.

This, again, confirmed that the Lord was speaking to me about going on the trip. I still was not seeing the finances for the trip and was questioning God about His plans. He then put the "icing on the cake," or should I say, "sealed the deal," by giving me the last confirmation through a commercial with the song "Let's Go, Grenada."

In conclusion, God provided all the finances that I needed for the mission trip to Grenada. On that trip, my heart was opened even more with compassion for people, especially for children. I realized that the Lord wanted to increase my compassion for people, giving me a greater love and desire to share the gospel with them. We spent eight days on the island, distributing hampers and doing outreaches in our assigned community.

Asking God to confirm His word for me has been a pattern that I have adopted over the years. This really helps me to be clear about something that God is saying to me, especially if it is in the area of making a major decision. There are two scriptures that I would use to correlate this truth: "The facts of the case must be established by the testimony of two or three witnesses" (Deuteronomy 19:15b) and "In the mouth of two or three witnesses shall every word be established" (2 Corinthians 13:1b).

Introduction to Life as a Career Missionary

The year 2009 arrived, and I did not know what to expect; however, during our New Year service, my pastor Osbert Williams prayed for me and said, "In the month of September, you will have to make a major decision so be in prayer from now." I obeyed the instructions and, on occasion, would pray for this major decision.

The month of September came, and the Lord directed me to resign my full-time job at the West Indies School of Theology (WIST). I started working at the institution in November 2006. After six months of working as the receptionist/clerk typist, I got promoted to the finance office where I worked as the director of business, managing the finances for the Bible school.

Before making this major decision of resigning, I prayed and fasted while waiting for the Lord to give me confirmation. The Lord gave me confirmation in a couple of ways, and I was now clear with the direction in which God was leading me. The final confirmation came from a friend through an email with a PowerPoint presentation that read, "Lord, help me to not remain where I am but help me to be where You want me to be." After reading this line, I felt a strong sense that this was what God wanted me to do. As a result, I was now at peace with my decision.

However, I did not know what my next step would be, but I kept hearing in my spirit the word *nations*. I obeyed God and resigned. However, my director was not pleased with my decision and did not immediately accept my resignation. He felt I was a good employee and did not see the need for me to leave the position since I did not have a clear plan in place for my next step. After a few days had passed, I met with my boss again, and this time, we had a more amicable conversation.

I shared with him that my season at the Bible school had changed, and I wanted to be able to move into my new season with Father God. My resignation letter was then accepted. I was no longer a full-time employee, but I instead worked part-time so that I could still assist with the work at the school while completing my studies.

One month after submitting my letter of resignation and having shifted my position, the Lord spoke to my spirit to sign up to do mission work on the *Logos Hope* ship. When I first heard these words, there was a tinge of fear in my heart. It seemed like this idea was now on the verge of becoming a reality. Nevertheless, I did the usual thing after sensing the Spirit of the Lord speaking to me. I asked Father God for confirmation. By the evening time, a former WIST student from Grenada contacted me and shared that she was now a missionary and travels from nation to nation in the Caribbean. I got excited in my spirit as I realized the Lord was giving me confirmation.

The following day during the Sunday morning service I attended, the pastor spoke about the all-sufficient God. She said, "If He says to do something, just obey, and He will work it out." As I heard these words in my spirit, I felt like this was another confirmation from Father God. Later that Sunday afternoon, I got a visit from a friend who was a missionary. I shared with her what the Lord was asking of me, and she remarked that she also felt in her spirit that God was leading me to serve with the ship ministry. She then prayed with me, and we believed together that God would continue to order my steps. She also shared some of her experiences with the ship ministry and gave me some relevant information about the application process.

My friend previously served on the *Doulos*, which is a sister ship to the *Logos Hope*. Truly, the Lord is faithful in all His ways, and most times, He sends us a forerunner to help guide us on the path that he has chosen for us.

Part of the process for applying to the ship ministry is to attend the local Global Missions Orientation (GMO). This training is conducted by Operation Mobilization (OM) Caribbean for all people from the Caribbean who is interested in joining the family of OM. This training is usually held either in Trinidad and Tobago, Barbados, or Jamaica.

In March 2010, I attended the training which was held aboard the *Logos Hope* ship in Jamaica. The training lasted one week and was not only very inspirational and informative but also very demanding. A key point mentioned in the training was for persons who felt called to full-time mission work to receive wise counsel from their pastors and any other trusted persons whom they respected. This counsel would help the individual gain the assurance that God was directing their steps as they move forward with the process.

Another important aspect of mission preparation is to incorporate a strong prayer team as well as consistent financial supporters. I never imagined living aboard a ship. The week spent aboard the *Logos Hope* was met with some measure of culture shock. I remembered asking God if He was sure this is where He wanted me to do missions. In my mind, I thought that I would go to a Spanish-speaking country to be involved in mission work. But instead, God wanted to send me to the nations via a ship called *Logos Hope*.

One month after the training in Jamaica, I got the good news that I was accepted into the Global Action (GA) Program. My commitment was to serve aboard the *Logos Hope* ship for two years, from September 2010 to September 2012. However, I had to leave in August to attend a two-week conference in the Netherlands, where all the new recruits would meet for orientation. This conference was the general mission's training for everyone who would join the larger family of OM within that particular year.

CHAPTER 3

First Mission aboard *Logos Hope*

Go Conference

After much preparation and packing, August 19, 2010, finally came. Now it was time to say my goodbyes. I was filled with mixed emotions, excited about this new chapter in my life, and also, I was experiencing sadness about leaving my family and friends behind. However, deep in my heart, there was a sense of peace as a result of my obedience to God. This was a huge step of faith for me, but I looked forward to going into the nations to fulfill God's purpose for my life.

The Go Conference in the Netherlands was held from August 24 to September 3, 2010. The purpose of this conference was to give practical and spiritual training to the new recruits. Some of the areas covered in the two-week training included sessions on experiencing God on a much deeper and personal level through prayer and worship, increasing one's vision for the needs and opportunities around the world, and having a better understanding of oneself and others (appreciating the differences in people). Focus was also given to developing a sense of appreciation for OM's core values, with an emphasis on working together as a team. Finally, there was cross-cultural training and orientation about the different fields where missionaries would be sent to serve.

There were approximately five hundred people present at the Go Conference, with fifty-five nationalities being represented. This was my first opportunity to visit Europe, as well as to interact with people from several different cultures and nations. I was the only representative from Trinidad and Tobago and the Caribbean. As a result, at times I felt a bit overwhelmed.

At the conference, we were encouraged to share our life experiences, pray with one another, and also to pray for one another. I enjoyed the times of sharing as this truly encouraged my faith. The storylines were different, but the theme running through the stories were all the same. The theme was that everyone said yes to the call of God to go on missions. Everyone was obedient and willing to give up their comfort zone to follow God's will for their lives. We were also taught to cultivate a quiet (shh) time with God.

There was also some time for informal fellowship where we had an opportunity to visit one of the villages. During the two weeks, some great friendships were formed, and everyone was enthusiastic about maintaining these friendships. At the end of the conference, some of the participants would be heading to the ship ministry while others would be heading to various countries, where they would serve with the land base ministries.

Pre-Ship Training

After the training in the Netherlands, we traveled to the Canary Islands where we met the ship. However, before embarking, we had to enroll in pre-ship training (PST). This is an integral part of the preparation for everyone joining the ship's ministry. Inclusive of myself, sixty people joined the *Logos Hope* ship ministry at that time.

Some topics covered during this training included information about the different departments aboard the ship. We also covered information about the importance of maintaining a positive attitude in serving God and others while reflecting on Christ. Emphasis was once again placed on working in teams and cultivating quiet times with God during the busy life aboard the ship. A major emphasis was placed on social policy (SP). This policy speaks to persons about the rule of not being allowed to enter a romantic relationship during the first year of service within the organization.

During the period of training, we were also placed into cell groups where we worked in teams and supported one another. There was no internet access at our location and therefore we were forced to have greater bonding time with each other. There was little time for sightseeing on the island because of the busy training schedule. Nevertheless, the beautiful scenery around our accommodation within the Las Palmas vicinity was thoroughly enjoyed.

Arrival Day

Arrival day on board the ship finally came on September 14, 2010. Most people were very excited for this special day. For some, it seemed like it was taking forever, and for others, we were just calm about the whole event. However, my excitement and emotional high began when we arrived at the port.

As we walked toward the ship, the crew members were cheering and waving their flags. Some were standing on deck 9 at the top of the ship, and others were on the quayside. My heart was really filled with joy when I saw the flag for my own country of Trinidad and Tobago being waived. As I saw the pretty colored flags, I thought of the countries that usually come together to represent their nations in the World Cup football competition. However, on this occasion, people from over fifty-one nationalities came together and waived their flags under the banner of Jesus Christ. This was really a great feeling, and I was happy to be a part of this auspicious occasion. I was grateful to God for providing me with this opportunity.

Over four hundred people were living on board when I joined the ship ministry. Among this number were four other Trinidadians who welcomed me very warmly. After the initial introductions aboard, we were treated with refreshments followed by a short tour of the ship. The ship was then scheduled to sail to Tenerife Island in three hours' time. As a result, we were also given a short lesson on some of the basic safety training procedures. There was a special dinner prepared for our new pre-ship training group, and we were also introduced to our ship families. Each new recruit joining the ship ministry was placed into a group called their "ship family." Once a week, this group would have dinner together and participate in many other fun activities just as a normal family.

The day after our arrival, we began the full basic safety training (BST), which is required for all persons living on board. This training was one week long. It was a very busy time, and the days were long, but we all made it through to the end. Practical training, which consisted of fire and water exercises, was also included. The water exercises were challenging for some of us mainly because we had to jump off the ship from deck 4 and swim to the lifeboat. After this time, we had to practice turning over a life raft and climbing into it.

On the last day of the training, we were given a written exam, and everyone was expected to pass. Passing this exam was very important to enable recruits to receive a certificate. This certificate would show proof of completion of the Safety of Life at Sea (SOLAS) training, which is mandatory for all persons living on ships.

Life on Board *Logos Hope*

I would usually start my mornings with breakfast at 7:00 a.m. then meet for community devotions from 7:45 a.m. to 8:30 a.m. After this time, I would begin my workday which ran from 9:00 a.m. to 5:00 p.m. Dinner was served between 5:30 p.m. and 7:00 p.m. The Sunday schedule on the ship started with breakfast at 8:00 a.m., followed by church service at 9:00 a.m. Lunch was served at noon, and I began my work from 1:00 p.m. to 8:00 p.m. My day off would usually be on Mondays and occasionally on Sundays. There would also be evening sessions such as worship night, ship family night, prayer night, and many other activities called "passion groups." All in all, life on the ship was always very busy.

What did my job entail? For the first four months, I worked with the visitors who came on board the ship to experience the bookfair. The bookfair would usually open from 10:00 a.m. to 10:00 p.m. I assisted the visitors at the information desk, cash desk, and also with customer service as they entered the bookfair located on deck 4. This area is called the Hope Experience Deck.

There were two minor challenges for me working on deck 4. The first challenge was the long hours standing on my feet at different locations. The second challenge was working the evening shift, which was from 4:00 p.m. to midnight. This was the first time in my life that I had to work late-night hours.

Back at home, I would usually be in my bed or asleep during this time. Some days, I had my low moments when I would complain and cry out to God telling Him about the long hours of standing. However, one night, as I started feeling tired and overwhelmed, instead of complaining, I decided to worship my way through the end of the shift. After this experience, I stopped complaining about my situation to God; instead, I asked Him for grace and strength to work through the night shifts.

As soon as my attitude toward my work changed, God allowed my position to be changed. I was promoted to work as the administrator in the bookfair office. My work time was now more stable from 9:00 a.m. to 5:00 p.m., and there was more flexibility with the working hours. I was now responsible for the data entry of all the books that arrived from the United Kingdom and the United States that were sold on the ship. Other responsibilities included setting up cash registers with the relevant currency for that nation. This would be done on the first day of arrival at the port of entry. I prepared the daily sales report for the bookfair and the customs report which was presented to the local customs authority. Whenever extra help was needed on a crowded day, I would gladly assist my team members at the cash register.

I enjoyed working on the cash register while interacting with the visitors during this time. Those were my main responsibilities on the ship for five days. On the sixth day, I would usually be involved in outreach ministry. This time of ministry focused on connecting with the local people either on the Hope

Experience Deck or onshore, at churches, schools, orphanages, or any other organization that teamed up with the ship's ministry.

I was very thankful to God for giving me the opportunity to serve in that capacity. I enjoyed the challenges of my new position even though it was demanding and very tiring at times. I also saw how God allowed me to use my past work experience as an accounts clerk to serve while being on the mission field.

Even though I was in the center of God's will and for the most part enjoying the journey, there were still challenges and low periods in which I felt overwhelmed. Most times during these low periods, I would become homesick. Whenever this happened, I would remind myself that I am about my Father's business, and He knows what is best for His children. I would always see God's hands taking me through, as He would encourage me with His Word, when I meditated on the scriptures, "For I know the plans I have for you," says the LORD. "They are plans for good and not for disaster, to give you a future and a hope" (Jeremiah 29:11).

My struggles with Father God were mainly internal as I was submitting to His will giving up my rights, personal desires, and independence. By committing to serve with an organization, you must also abide by their rules and guidelines, whereby submitting yourself to the way things are done. This was another area in which I learned about submitting my will to God's will and purpose.

One example of giving up my personal desire was having to share cabin space with another person. After living independently for many years, this adjustment was very difficult. Once again, God used this as an area for growth, where I had to learn tolerance and acceptance in living with people from different cultures. The fruit of the Spirit was certainly developed as I learned the lessons of love, patience, kindness, gentleness, and self-control.

Giving up my independence was one of my major challenges aboard the ship. There were many times when I missed being at home and experiencing the freedom I was accustomed to. Life on the ship was fully structured, and everything was planned out for you. Father God desires that we develop in our character, and He chooses the best place for this development to take place. For me, the *Logos Hope* ship community was this place.

Throughout one's commitment on the ship, there are set training sessions that occur every six months. These sessions are geared toward helping crew members process the emotional stresses that may occur at these points. I can totally attest to the emotional stress that occurred at these points during my time on board. In the first four to six months, I became more settled and adjusted to life aboard the ship. At the end of my first year, I was at a low point; however, after attending the session called "Life Direction Chat," my focus on God's will for my life and ministry once again returned. After this session, I felt encouraged and strengthened in my spirit and emotions.

Season of Pruning

The fifteen to eighteen months aboard the *Logos* was the most challenging period for me. During that time, I became very exhausted emotionally, physically, mentally, and spiritually. The process of renewing my strength during that period was very slow. However, day by day, I continued the journey pressing through my low moments as I encouraged myself in the Lord.

I spent two days praying and fasting, seeking the Lord and asking Him for strength. After this time, I got an invitation from the events office to be a featured speaker at a lady's event where two hundred ladies from the Philippines were expected to attend. I told the events coordinator that I would respond to her at a later date. I then went to Father God inquiring about His will in this situation. I told Him I needed strength and did not feel like speaking now, but if it was His will, then I would speak. I felt the Lord say He wanted me to speak at the event titled "Staying Connected to the Vine" taken from John 15. I then confirmed with the events coordinator that I would speak at the event.

As I started reading the scriptures and did some research on the Internet, I realized that the Word of God was speaking directly into my spirit. God used this message to really encourage my heart, as He revealed to me that I was in a season of pruning. He was preparing me to bring forth more fruit for Him as He was taking me to a new level of spiritual growth.

After sharing at the event, several ladies said to me they were tremendously blessed by the message; so much so in the following week, one of the attendees from the conference contacted someone from the ship, requesting for me to visit her home cell group. This woman wanted me to share the same message with her group of ladies, hoping that the message would also be a blessing to them. Once again, I felt the Lord say to me to go and share His Word with the women in the cell group. This time of sharing turned out to be a great blessing not just to the group but also to me. God not only encouraged my spirit during that time, but He also allowed these lovely Filipino people to bless me in a tangible way. I stood in awe of God's faithfulness toward me despite my shortcomings and weaknesses.

Little by little, my strength was being regained, but I was still in a place where I just felt numb before God. I was only focusing on the present moment, just taking daily steps without thinking about what lay ahead. As I continued my journey dealing with low periods and feelings of emotional numbness, I fell ill on the last day in the port of Manila. I slept in my cabin for the entire day and into the night. On that night, the ship sailed from the Port of Manila to Subic Bay, Philippines. The following day, I felt a little better but still had a headache. Two days after this, I noticed that I had some red spots on my body, which turned out to be chicken pox. Because of this, I had to spend eight days confined to my cabin. This was a very painful experience with much discomfort, but I thank God for His presence during my pain. I was also encouraged by a few crew members with cards sent to my cabin, letting me know they were praying for me. God knew I needed all the prayers I could have gotten during that time because I was unable to pray for myself amid my pain and discomfort.

This was not an easy period for me, but God encouraged me from Psalm 121 (KJV). This is a familiar passage of scripture that I could recite, so I just kept reading it casually. By the middle of the week, as I continued to read, the Holy Spirit illuminated verse 7 to me, which says, "The LORD shall preserve you from all evil: he shall preserve your soul." I felt Father God saying, "My daughter, I allowed you to be afflicted so that I could preserve you and your soul. I want to show you how much I love you, and I want you to learn to rest in Me and My love for you."

I experienced an overwhelming feeling of God's love being poured out on me during this time. As my heart, soul, and body experienced healing, my attitude toward God changed. My attitude toward God had not been in the right place. I was somewhat angry and upset with God as a result of all the pain and hurt I felt during my season of pruning. Because of this, my heart started to harbor seeds of bitterness toward my current situation. Father God encouraged me to continue trusting His will and plan for my life.

I tried my best to keep my faith and to trust God, but there were times when my faith wavered, especially when I became tired. Nevertheless, after spending those eight days confined to my cabin, I was able to testify to God's love, His sustaining power, and His faithfulness. Father God restored and refreshed my soul during my time of affliction. This encouraged me to continue my journey as "I pressed toward the mark for the prize of the high calling of God in Christ Jesus" (Philippians 3:14 KJV). My allegiance toward a faithful God had increased because of His love revealed to me during this season.

After this experience, I started seeing afflictions in a different light. I saw how God would sometimes use our seasons of affliction to protect us. But more importantly, He uses this time to strengthen our faith and comfort us so that we can comfort others during their seasons of affliction. "He comforts us in all our troubles so that we can comfort others. When they are troubled, we will be able to give them the same comfort God has given us" (2 Corinthians 1:4).

Life-Changing Experiences

Despite a few challenges of having some low periods and internal battles which were fought and won, I would not trade for anything the knowledge and experience gained while living aboard the ship. One of my greatest highlights was having the world map come alive. I interacted with people daily from different places in the world. Some of these places I have only previously heard or read about and, in some cases, seen on television. We shared our stories with one another during mealtime while working together or during our ministry days. We learned a great deal about one another's culture. This experience further enhanced my worldview. I would not have had this opportunity if I did not say yes to God's will. I felt honored to be an ambassador sent by the Lord to the nations, sharing the good news of Jesus Christ.

I was blessed to have cabin mates from three countries—Australia, Chile, and France. I look forward to visiting these countries in the near future. I also made great connections with lovely families in some of the countries we visited. I truly believe that God gave me the favor to connect with these families. I would often pray for divine connections before we arrived in a country, and I can testify that in each port, this prayer was answered.

Most people we meet during our visits to the various countries were always amazed when we shared that everyone aboard the *Logos Hope* was a volunteer, including the captain and engineers. No one received an income. They were always encouraged to hear that so many people both young and old were willing to give up their comfort zone to do God's will. This fact has been one of the biggest testimonies of the ship ministry.

Everyone who lives on board the ship takes pride in sharing some of the facts about their country. Many local people from certain countries never heard about the Caribbean. I used every opportunity when connecting with local people to share about Trinidad and Tobago. On my ministry days, I often used a world map to showcase the location of the Caribbean Sea. I also used my country's flag to represent my beautiful country. Some people were amazed to hear about the natural resources that the twin island of Trinidad and Tobago are blessed with.

Historical Ports

Because our Heavenly Father created us, He knows the things we like, especially those things that would bring pleasure to us. He also knows the things we do not like and do not desire. Just like in a normal relationship, the man would woo the woman whom he likes to get to know her more intimately. So too, God pursues us in the same manner, but His overall agenda is for us to know Him more intimately. "And this is the way to have eternal life—to know you, the only true God, and Jesus Christ, the one you sent to earth" (John 17:3).

There is a difference in the relationship pursuit from the man's standpoint. In the initial stages of the courtship between a man and a woman, the man may only do things to make the woman happy. However, God's approach does not only include giving us things that we like and that would make us happy. God is also interested in developing our character as was mentioned before when I talked about the fruit of the Spirit. God desires that we enjoy our journey on earth, and at the same time, His overall purpose for our lives takes precedence over our need for continual happiness.

Father God knows that traveling, sightseeing, and interacting with people of different cultural backgrounds are some of my greatest delights. God wooed me unto Himself as He enabled me to visit the historical ports in the countries Malta, Egypt, and Lebanon.

During the first six months of my journey aboard *Logos Hope*, my faith in God increased. I was totally out of my comfort zone, and there were certain things that I did not particularly like but had to get accustomed too. However, being able to walk on the soil of these historical countries, which is written in my Bible, increased my love and appreciation for the Lord.

After these experiences, the stories in the Bible came alive to me even more than before.

One story that can be found in the book of Acts speaks about the apostle Paul's journey to Rome and being shipwrecked on his way to the island of Malta. I was privileged to visit Saint Paul's shipwreck church. We were able to observe an annual procession, which commemorated Paul's visit to the island. After the procession, there were fireworks, the ringing of church bells, and the firing of cannons that could be heard throughout the entire city. It was evident that the people of Malta appreciated the history of Paul's visit to their country because, after two thousand years, the celebrations continue. The ship's visit to this country was very special to the entire crew because of its historical significance. Our ministry was very well received in Malta as we were able to encourage believers and pray for unity in the church of Jesus Christ.

A team of us had the opportunity to visit the city of Birgu in Malta. We attended a local festival called Birgu Fest. At that festival, we were able to share some of our ship experiences as well as play games and other activities with the children.

A few months after our visit to Malta, the team received an email from our host at the Birgu Fest. He shared his testimony of how we impacted his life during our visit, and this is what he wrote:

> *Merry late Christmas and New Year's wishes from Malta! You're in my prayers many times as you sail around the world! I have to tell you a secret—when you were here in Malta and we did that activity with the school children, I didn't know what to expect. I thought I would not be good for it, or that I would find people who would not be easy to work with, or*

something like that. On the contrary, it was a real pleasure to work with you, and it was an experience I'll never forget! Most of all, the thing that made the biggest effect on me was the immense amount of Christian faith which all you guys possess and which you are not afraid to show! It made me realise that there is still a God that loves us up there, although I had lost him a long time ago. I really wanna thank you for the experience, because even though maybe you don't realise it, you guys helped me a lot, by your example, at a time in my life when I was going through some rough times. I found my faith again, and this helped me start enjoying life again. Today I'm a much happier person! :) Thanks a lot! May your voyages always be blessed by God, and kept always free of trouble. Good luck! Cheers!!

Andy from Malta

This email really encouraged our hearts because we saw that our faith in God was observed by others when we were not even aware of it. Hence, it's the reason we should always have a Christlike attitude in whatever we do.

We visited two other historical countries in December 2010. First, we visited Egypt and then Lebanon. Our time in Egypt was very short where we spent eight days. The crew members had limited ministry opportunities in this port. We were given the opportunity to connect with local children at an Orthodox Church; however, because of the language barrier, this proved to be a challenge. Nevertheless, the team enjoyed the time spent with the children. The highlights for the ship's community in Egypt were being able to visit the Great Pyramid of Giza, see the Nile River, and have the experience of a camel ride at the pyramids. This camel ride experience was then crossed off my bucket list.

In Lebanon, we spent eighteen days, which included the Christmas season. Here, we had more opportunities to connect with the locals. During our stay in the city of Lebanon, it was very cold, especially in the evenings and early mornings. In certain areas, some of the mountaintops were covered with snow. Several adventurous crew members made trips to the mountains to experience the snow. Some months after our time in Lebanon, as I read from the book of Jeremiah, I came upon the scripture that talked about the snow on the mountaintop in Lebanon. This was another "wow" moment for me. Once again, the scriptures came alive because I remembered seeing these mountains with my own eyes. "Does the snow ever disappear from the mountaintops of Lebanon? Do the cold streams flowing from those distant mountains ever run dry?" (Jeremiah 18:14). Another beautiful sight in Lebanon that is very popular, which can also be found in the Bible, is the famous cedar trees.

One of my highlights for this port was being able to connect with the local women. I had the opportunity to be one of the hosts at a women's conference on board the ship. This event was geared toward encouraging and esteeming women from different religious backgrounds. There were also other opportunities for ministry at the local high schools and a kids' club where we were able to minister to the children through sports and other events. I also had the privilege to visit the oldest and first school for blind and disabled people in the Middle East. On my day off, I took some time to visit the ancient city of Byblos, which is known as one of the oldest continuously inhabited cities in the world.

"For since the world began, no ear has heard and no eye has seen a God like you, who works for those who wait for him!" (Isaiah 64:4).

"That is what the Scriptures mean when they say, no eye has seen, no ear has heard, and no mind has imagined what God has prepared for those who love him" (1 Corinthians 2:9).

These two scriptures encapsulate the heart of God as it relates to those who love Him and wait for Him. He works on their behalf, and He desires to wow them, not only in this life but also for all of eternity.

After our time in Lebanon, we sailed through the Suez Canal and then through the Red Sea as the ship made her way to the Arabian Peninsula. Yes, this was the same Red Sea mentioned in the Bible that Moses parted for the children of Israel to cross over to the other side. "It was by faith that the people of Israel went right through the Red Sea as though they were on dry ground. But when the Egyptians tried to follow, they were all drowned" (Hebrews 11:29).

Our New Year celebration for 2011 was ushered in while sailing through the Red Sea. We did not have the usual fireworks, but instead, we had the open heavens covered with beautiful stars lighting up the sky. This was a very memorable occasion for me. I stood in awe of God for who He is and for all the experiences He allowed me to have during the first few months of my journey aboard *Logos Hope*.

CHAPTER 4

Second Mission aboard *Logos Hope*

Extended Commitment

"You can make many plans, but the LORD's purpose will prevail" (Proverbs 19:21). A few days before my one-year mark aboard, I had a dream where I was back at home in Trinidad and Tobago when I said to someone, "I have to meet the ship for the nineteenth." The next morning when I awoke, I said to myself, *That was a strange dream.* However, on the following day, a group of us were having lunch when one of the guys from Germany stated that he had five more months before his commitment ended. I then shared that I have one more year before my commitment ends. At that point, one of the young ladies from Saint Vincent looked at me and said very convincingly, "You will be extending."

In my mind, I smiled to myself because I immediately remembered the dream from the night before. Within one week, several people conversed with me about extending their time on board the ship. I then said to Father God, "I do not know what to make of all this talk about extension of commitment because I do not have any desire to extend my time aboard the ship." I then felt a strong conviction from God in my spirit, telling me to commit for another year. I shared this revelation from God with one of my prayer partners. I said to her, "If God wants me to extend, He will use someone from the personnel department to confirm what He revealed to me because I am not willing to ask."

As the weeks and months continued, so too did the random questions and conversations about my extension on board the ship. My response to everyone was, "I am waiting on God to confirm His will for my life in this area." God then confirmed His will for me through the Word as I read two portions of scripture on the same day at different times. Firstly, I read, "Watch out! Remember the three years I was with you—my constant watch and care over you night and day, and my many tears for you" (Acts 20:31).

Secondly, I read, "Then three years later I went to Jerusalem to get to know Peter, and I stayed with him for fifteen days" (Galatians 1:18). The two abovementioned scriptures both highlighted a three-year period. This word of knowledge from the scriptures solidified for me that after my two-year commitment, the Lord wanted me to extend for another year. However, I was still struggling in my heart to accept this fact; nevertheless, I continued to pray, "Father, please help me to say yes to Your will." These words are similar to Jesus's words when He said, "Nevertheless not my will but your will be done" (Luke 22:42).

Six months after the initial talk of extending my time on board the ship, the training manager came to me and asked if

I would be extending. He wanted me to be a part of his team in the training department. I told him I know that God wants me to commit for another year, but I still wasn't clear in which area He wanted me to work. After this conversation, I began thinking about what it would be like working in the training department and if I was equipped to do this job. I then went to my cabin, and upon checking my inbox, there were emails from two different people. Both emails encouraged me to see God as my strength and believe that He would give me the grace to do His will. Once again, I took this as confirmation that God wanted me to work in the training department. I was now at peace and knew that Father God had settled the matter as it related to extending for an additional year. I was also certain that he wanted me to work in the training department.

Furlough

After completing one year and eleven months aboard the ship, I took leave and returned to Trinidad and Tobago. The ship was in a dry dock in the port of Subic Bay, Philippines. I spent eight weeks at home. This time was extremely busy as I connected with family, friends, faithful supporters, and local churches. I had the opportunity to preach at the churches that supported me for the initial two years of my missionary journey. I was thankful that whenever I ministered the Word of God, many lives were impacted by the move of the Spirit. I was equally blessed and challenged to continue practicing what I preached.

I had a spontaneous teaching session at my alma mater, the West Indies School of Theology (WIST). I was invited by the president to fill in for one of the lecturers who was absent. My teaching session was based on a missionary's life and work.

During my time at home, I also celebrated my birthday with family, attended my grandmother's eighty-fourth birthday party, and got the opportunity to be at one of my sisters' wedding. After expending all this energy, I visited the island of Tobago where I got some much-needed rest before heading back to the ship on October 28, 2012.

New Season on Board

As I left my home for the second time in two years, I once again had mixed emotions heading back into the nations. I knew this was God's will for my life, and I would often remind myself of the prayer that Jesus prayed in the garden of Gethsemane, where He said, "Nevertheless not my will but your will be done" (Luke 22:42). Despite the quoted words above, I was still battling in my mind about God's will of being on the ship for another year. This all happened during the initial week of my return. Finally, I decided to surrender and trust God in what He was doing and what He was preparing me for in the future. I was determined to make the most of this next chapter of my life.

After traveling for two days from the Caribbean back to the Philippines, I needed some extra rest because of jet lag, so I requested two vacation days. After this time of rest, I was now ready to become acquainted with my new office and the new team. It was a pleasure to see some of the familiar faces who I left on board the ship. My heart was encouraged by the number of people who expressed their appreciation for my return to the ship ministry. I also had to get acquainted with ninety-three new faces and names of new recruits who joined the ship while I was at home. Most people from my pre-ship group completed their commitment and left the ship except for eight of us who extended our time on board.

As a "second termer," I had a greater responsibility to continue being an example to the junior recruits. I started my assignment of working in the training department as one of the ministry trainers. One of my main responsibilities was overseeing the STEP-pers. STEP stands for *Short-Term Exposure Program*. These are recruits who join the ship for three months to receive an introduction to life on board. The hope is that as they get exposure to the ministry on board the *Logos*, the Lord will lead them to become interested in the two-year mission program. I really enjoyed working with the STEP-pers. This experience was very meaningful because I was able to disciple young people and prepare them for ministry involvement on board the ship and in the local communities.

Some of my other responsibilities were leading the children's ministry, which included Sunday school. I also lead pre-ship training sessions for new recruits and assisted with some of the general training for the entire ship's community. During my initial weeks in the training department, I was still involved in handing over administrative duties for the bookfair. This work could not have been completed beforehand due to the nine months extended dry dock, which affected the departments' general operations.

As I entered this second phase of the ship's life, I continued to draw strength from Father God. I knew He was the one Who placed me in this new position and promised to give me the grace that I needed to complete my assignment.

Cambodia—Arrival of New Recruits

In February and September of each year, there is an intake of new recruits on board the ship. The training team is responsible to meet the group of new recruits before the ship arrives at its destination to prepare the accommodations for their arrival.

Six team members including myself disembarked the *Logos Hope* ship in the port of Hong Kong and traveled overnight via Singapore to Cambodia where we met the new recruits. Even though some of the long layovers can be exhausting, I always enjoy every opportunity to travel via airplane, especially having a window seat.

There were two free days before the arrival of the new recruits, and during this time, we had the opportunity to visit the Genocide Museum in the capital city of Phnom Penh. I was able to learn a little more about the history of Cambodia, which is a very sad one. The country is still trying to recover from the memory of the Vietnam War as well as the extreme Marxist Khmer Rouge incident in which the genocide took place. It was very heartbreaking to listen to what the Cambodians endured for four years of Marxist oppression. Most people are very sensitive about the whole event, and as a result, they seldom speak about it.

Our day started very early with the arrival of the new recruits. We got to the airport before their flight arrived. In this February intake, forty-seven single people joined the crew, along with a family of four, which included two young children. My main responsibilities for the team were managing the finances and leading some of the training sessions which I thoroughly enjoyed. It was also fun leading one of the fellowship groups while getting acquainted with the new recruits.

Fellowship groups are geared toward helping recruits to bond in smaller numbers with persons of similar age ranges as they participate in different fun activities. Our day would usually start at 7:00 a.m., and on some occasions, we would end around 10:00 p.m. The schedule was very hectic for everyone, and halfway through the time in Cambodia, the new recruits were a bit exhausted. Some recruits suffered from information overload because of the many training sessions they experienced, firstly in Germany and then in Cambodia. However, the highlights for everyone in the group along with the trainers were the seafront view hotel accommodation and the exceptional food that was served.

Some of the new recruits from the pre-ship training (PST) group were blessed in more ways than one because they got the opportunity to welcome the ship as she sailed into the port of Sihanoukville, Cambodia. This experience was also very special for me because it was my first time witnessing the *Logos Hope* ship sailing into a dock. Usually, I would be on board the ship as she sailed into the port.

Presentation Team in Japan

Logos Hope ship has an annual dry dock as part of maritime requirements for passenger vessels. This is a period where the vessel would be docked in the shipyard receiving routine maintenance work for a period of four to six weeks.

During the dry dock for 2013, I was asked to travel to Japan for one month on a presentation team sharing about the ship ministry. This team consisted of four members, and I was assigned to be the team leader. We left the ship on April 1 and traveled to Japan via South Korea. After spending the night at the international airport in Japan, we boarded a domestic flight early the next morning. Our destination was OM Japan's office where we met our hosts—the field leaders for Japan. During our stay in Japan, we visited five cities. We spent the first week in the city of Kanazawa. We then traveled by car to Nagoya, where we spent the second week. The final two weeks were spent between Tokyo, Chiba, and Yokohama. Our goals were to promote the ship's ministry and raise financial support to purchase two new vans. These vehicles would assist the ship's personnel with transportation while docked in different countries.

During our time in the five cities of Japan, the team gave presentations in church meetings, high schools, international schools, Bible schools, and English cafés. I also preached at one of the local churches and was thankful to God for this opportunity. Sharing the Gospel in different nations of the world continued to be a very meaningful part of my experience. Christians represent only 1 percent of Japan's population as most of the people practice Buddhism and Shintoism.

Our visit to Japan was at the beginning of spring. This is a very special time because the cherry blossom trees are in full bloom. These trees turn white and look like they are covered with snow. One afternoon during our free time, we visited one of the national parks and enjoyed seeing some of Japan's beauty, and by extension, God's lovely creation. Our time in Japan doing ministry was very busy and totally enjoyable.

Two weeks before leaving for Japan, I was asked to be the personal assistant (PA) for the managing director of the ship. This was a huge surprise for me because I did not anticipate working in that capacity on board the ship. It was now March, and I enjoyed working in the training department and was expecting to be there until October 2013, which was my scheduled end of commitment aboard the ship.

God, however, had other plans for my life. He always prepares us for what He is about to do. The night before I was asked to change my job, I was reading through my journal and came upon an entry that I wrote before leaving Trinidad. A friend of mine prayed for me and said, "You will not only be involved in training, but this is where God is placing you so that He can take you to the next place."

At that time, I did not fully understand what my friend said to me, but I made a note in my journal and forgot about it. After being asked to be placed in this new position, I immediately remembered what I read in my journal and knew this was of God. Nevertheless, I still prayed and asked God for another confirmation, which He affirmed. Having said yes to this change of job also meant that I had to extend my time for another four months until February 2014.

Loss of My Maternal Grandmother

After returning to the ship from Japan, I rested for two days before starting my new job as a personal assistant to the director. However, it was a bit difficult to settle back into life on board. Three days into my new job, I received the sad news that my grandmother Mildred Isidore (a.k.a. Farfam, Wham, or my special pet name Farmfy) passed away because of a heart attack. This was a very difficult time for my mother, Victoria Isidore, because my grandmother passed away on her birthday.

It was an equally difficult time for the rest of my relatives and also for me because I was very close to my grandmother being the first grandchild in the family. For the first twelve years of my life, I lived with my grandmother and extended family. At the beginning of high school, I moved in with my mother and younger brother Shaun. I, however, looked forward to spending weekends with my extended family, especially granny who favored and loved me unconditionally. She knew that soup was one of my favorite meals, and most times, she would prepare soup during my weekend visits. My grandmother was also the person responsible for giving me the name Susan, which is of Hebrew origin meaning "graceful lily."

After praying about going home for the funeral, I felt the Lord saying, "Don't go home." At that time, I felt very helpless because I could not be at home to support my mom and other relatives. I believed that God knew this was the best decision for me because it would have been too stressful to travel home and return to the ship in a short space of time.

The weeks that followed my grandmother's passing were very difficult. I started feeling emotionally tired and broken as I was trying to make sense of what God was doing in my life. One night, as I cried out to God, I asked Him, "Why did You take away my grandmother at this time, knowing how dear she was to me and that one of my desires was for her to be present at my wedding?" I then had this overwhelming feeling that I should speak to someone to help with the grieving process.

The next morning during devotions, the director announced that we had a visiting counselor on board, and she was available to meet with people. God is so faithful in always meeting our needs even before we ask Him. Later that same evening, I met with the counselor and shared where I was emotionally and what I was feeling. She listened to me intently as I poured out my heart and then encouraged me to stop telling God about my problems and just give Him my burdens. The counselor then prayed for me and encouraged me to take some time away from work, which she felt would further help with the grieving process.

After sharing with the counselor, I then went to my cabin and picked up a book to read. I had taken this book with me to Japan, but for some reason, I could not find time to complete the reading. I am the type of person who would usually read an entire book from cover to cover before starting a new one. I was, however, now determined to read the book before returning it to my fellow crew member.

That same night as I continued reading from where I left off, the author spoke about a lady he met in Egypt. This lady's story was about losing her grandmother when she was thirteen years old. The lady told him that, as a young child, she was raised by her grandmother who became a major influence in her life. During that difficult season of her grandmother's passing, she became angry and upset with God. She asked God why He took her grandmother away during the time she was experiencing other major challenges in her life. The lady explained that some time after her grandmother's passing, she met with a pastor to receive counseling. The pastor said to her, "Don't you understand? God has stripped you away from everything you know so that all you have left is to rely on Him." Wow, these words had such a great impact on me because they spoke so clearly about my current situation. These words were quite similar to what I spoke to Father God about the night before.

As I concluded reading through that part of the story, I felt the peace of God in my heart and mind. I do believe that God used this story to answer my question about the loss of my grandmother. Once again, I saw how God has our seasons and times in His hands. I started reading this book while we were in Japan, but it took longer than usual for me to complete it. God had orchestrated this delay because He knew the timing at which I would have needed to read this story. Father God also used the scripture from Psalm 23 to encourage my heart during this low period of my journey.

> The LORD is my shepherd; I have all that
> I need. He lets me rest in green meadows; he
> leads me beside peaceful streams. He renews
> my strength. He guides me along right paths,

bringing honor to his name. Even when I walk through the darkest valley, I will not be afraid, for you are close beside me. Your rod and your staff protect and comfort me. You prepare a feast for me in the presence of my enemies. You honor me by anointing my head with oil. My cup overflows with blessings. Surely your goodness and unfailing love will pursue me all the days of my life, and I will live in the house of the LORD forever.

The words of this Psalm reassured me of God's love and comfort during the months following the death of my grandmother and my stepmom who passed away a few weeks after my grandmother. God knew that I would have liked to be home to support and comfort my mom during her time of grief. I would have also liked to be at home to extend this same comfort to my dad and younger brother Ovil during their time of grief. But God directed otherwise because He knew how broken I would have been during that time. He also revealed to me that He was using this time of grief to draw my relatives closer to Him.

I am thankful to God for ordering our every step because He knows what is best for us and when to make the necessary changes in our lives. I felt that my change in job was the best outcome during the passing of my grandmother. My job working in the training department was more people oriented, and this took a lot from my "emotional tank" because of my role as a member care for the STEP-pers. In addition to this, I also prepared and executed training sessions for crew members. My new job as a personal assistant to the director was more task oriented. This position allowed me to go through my grieving process much easier because my secretarial duties gave me more time alone. During this time, the Holy Spirit was able to strengthen me mentally, emotionally, and spiritually.

My new boss, the late Lloyd Nicholas, was very gracious and accommodating in allowing me to take the necessary time off. Arrangements were made for me to leave the ship, and I stayed at a nearby hotel for a few days. It was a very nice and relaxing time just being away from the busy schedule of the ship's life. God also used this time to give me closure with my grandmother by giving me a beautiful dream about her.

In the dream, it seemed as though I was walking to the top of a hill, and when I got there, my grandmother was already there. She looked very youthful and radiant, dressed in a laced wedding gown with a matching head piece. As I got closer to her, she outstretched her hand to give me a white-laced blouse. At first, I hesitated to take it, but then I reached out my hand to receive the gift. As soon as I took the blouse from her hand, she leaped off the mountain-top, flew into the air, and gradually faded into the clouds. She then looked back at me and smiled, and we both blew each other a kiss.

During the dream, there was such a sense of peace in the midst of my grandmother and me. It appeared as if we were both saying our final goodbyes to each other. I am thankful to God that I was at home the previous year in October, where we celebrated my grandmother's eighty-fourth birthday. This was the last birthday that she spent on earth. God is faithful even when we do not fully understand what He is doing and when it relates to the experience of loss and pain. Isaiah says it this way: "Don't be afraid, for I am with you. Don't be discouraged, for I am your God. I will strengthen you and help you. I will hold you up with my victorious right hand" (Isaiah 41:10).

In the early days of my relationship with Father God, as my spiritual eyes were opened, one of the things that He showed me was the reality that generational blessings exist and so, too, do generational curses. This fact caused me to look closely into my family's lineage as I observed some of the generational blessings that I benefited from and some of the curses that still existed.

One of these generational curses was family strife between mother and daughter. Thankfully, God has given all believers the power and authority through the blood of Jesus Christ to overcome every generational curse that may have been inherited into their lives. I would like to conclude this section by testifying that God has broken the generational curse of family strife between mother and daughter in our lineage. I am thankful that He restored the relationship between my mother and my grandmother before she passed away, and He has also restored the relationship between my mother and me.

Change in Perspective

I was humbled by what God was doing in my life aboard the ship. Working in the position of administrative assistant to a director might be seen by some as a very influential job. As a result, when people asked me how I felt working as the personal assistant to the managing director, I would say, "This job is just a higher level of servanthood. Instead of serving the general community, I will now be serving the director of the ship."

There is a story behind working in the capacity of a secretary. I believe God wanted to change my perspective as it relates to this profession. As a young child, I aspired to become a secretary in my adult life. During my time in high school, I worked diligently to accomplish this goal. For some students, choosing subjects for final exams was done in the third year, and for others in the fourth year of high school. I chose my subjects in the fourth year. Anyone pursuing a career in secretarial work would know that typing is one of the main subjects required. However, because of a setback in my registration process, I was unable to be admitted into the typing class.

After graduating from high school, I attended a secretarial school for one year, which was funded by my mother. There, I pursued typing along with other subjects, all to accomplish my goal of becoming a secretary. I give honor to my mother for providing for me and my younger brother during our childhood. As a single parent, she worked assiduously to ensure that all our needs were met, especially in the area of our education. This gave us a foundation for our future.

I thoroughly enjoyed my studies at the secretarial school and looked forward to using my skills in the world of work. The school was located on the lower level of a two-story building while the upper level housed an accounting firm. Being my usual friendly self, I made friends with the secretary at the firm. Upon completion of my studies, the secretary asked her boss if I could work as her assistant for a small stipend. The boss agreed, and I accepted the position. I saw this as an opportunity to get work experience while putting into practice what was learned at the secretarial school.

As I worked closely with the secretary, I realized that I didn't particularly like some of the things that were practiced. For example, on a few occasions, the truth would be conveniently altered on behalf of the boss. It appears she had to be at his *beck and call*—being entirely subservient to him or being responsive to his slightest request. This observation caused me to despise the idea of being a secretary. I enjoyed using my administrative skills but no longer wanted to pursue the profession. Instead, I changed my focus and worked using my analytical skills in the area of accounting.

When the door was opened for me to work as the personal assistant (PA) to the managing director, I felt God saying to me, "You need to change your perspective on being a secretary and what it means to be subservient because I have created you to serve one another, as this brings fulfillment in your life." After this insight from God, my perspective changed. I began seeing a secretary as someone in a position of influence who has the great opportunity to serve the leader and others. I can attest to this new insight because I saw it materialize first-hand in my role as a personal assistant to the managing director. My desire for writing was also birthed as I sat at this desk typing a number of reports for my boss. I took pleasure in serving him in this capacity as he served the community, and we both enjoyed working with each other.

In the book of Mathew, Jesus spoke to His disciples about the whole attitude of serving others.

In *Mathew 20:20–26,*

> Then the mother of James and John, the sons of Zebedee, came to Jesus with her sons. She knelt respectfully to ask a favor. "What is your request?" he asked. She replied, "In your Kingdom, please let my two sons sit in places of honor next to you, one on your right and the other on your left." But Jesus answered by saying to them, "You don't know what you are asking! Are you able to drink from the bitter cup of suffering I am about to drink?" "Oh yes," they replied, "we are able!" Jesus told them, "You will indeed drink from my bitter cup. But I have no right to say who will sit on my right or my left. My Father has prepared those places for the ones he has chosen." When the ten other disciples heard what James and John had asked, they were indignant. But Jesus called them together and said, "You know that the rulers in this world lord it over their people, and officials flaunt their

authority over those under them. But among you it will be different. Whoever wants to be a leader among you must be your servant."

Farewell Testimony

At the end of one's time serving aboard the *Logos*, the opportunity is given to share a five-minute farewell testimony. I would like to share with you my farewell testimony at the end of my three and a half years.

Dear supporters and prayer partners,

Greetings in the wonderful name of our Lord and Savior Jesus Christ!

"I have fought a good fight, I have finished my course, I have kept the faith" (2 Timothy 4: 7).

The time has come for me to say goodbye to *Logos Hope*, and it is my pleasure to share my farewell testimony with you. I would like to sum up my time aboard *Logos Hope* in three words, which are *death*, *life*, and *faith*. *Death*. I had to die to my will so that God's will could be done in my life, die to my flesh in that I had to choose to give up my rights just as Jesus did when He gave up His rights, die to my pride and my independence. *Life*. As I died to my flesh, Christ's life was seen in me, and this brought life and encouragement to the people around me. This also encouraged me to keep pressing forward with God. *Faith*. My faith in God and my relationship with God grew tremendously during the last three and a half years. There were some challenges, but in the end, this brought me closer to God. I learned to trust Him even more with my life. One of the greatest things God taught me, especially during the hard times, was that He always works everything out for my good and for His glory.

I joined the *Logos* ship in the Canary Islands with an amazing group of people called PST Las Palmas in September 2010. My time aboard was mixed with many blessings, challenges, high times, and low times. I thank God for giving me the opportunity to serve in different capacities, such as the administrator in the bookfair, coleading the *Logos Hope* intensive training (LIT), ministry trainer in the training department, PA to the director, and service desk attendant. I also worked for brief periods in some of the other departments during the Subic Bay dry dock. This gave me greater respect and appreciation for the work that is done in all departments. I never saw myself working in some of these positions, but God knows me more than I know myself. He saw it fit to open these doors so that my life could bring glory to Him as I served. I enjoyed serving in each position where God allowed me to use my existing skills and talents, and in other areas, He birthed new gifts and sharpened some of my spiritual gifts.

Some highlights

➢ Sharing God's love in some amazing places, in total nineteen countries and forty-seven ports

➢ Leading a presentation team/traveling team in Japan

➢ Being a part of five challenge teams (land-based living)

➢ Coleading *Logos Hope* intensive training (LIT) and seeing tremendous growth in the ten participants after nine weeks

➢ Leading Friday night Caribbean prayer meeting

➢ Being a part of kids' ministry and teaching the children in Sunday school

➢ Being able to read many great books, which have been my biggest mentor aboard together with the Holy Spirit

➢ Being able to mentor and coach some of the younger ladies and see them grow in confidence in who they are and also in their relationship with God

➢ Getting to know and meet many people from around the world

➢ Being a trainer for my one and only PST—Sihanoukville (Cambodia)

Some low lights

➢ Being ill with chicken pox in March 2012 during a stressful time

➢ Missed having my own room and space and being frustrated with some of the systems aboard

➢ Losing two significant people in my family in 2013—my grandmother and my stepmom

➢ Having to say goodbye to friends each changeover was emotionally draining

I wish to thank

➢ GOD for sustaining me over the last few years. He has been faithful to me, and I have more confidence in Him that when He calls us, He equips us and qualifies us for the task at hand.

➢ All my faithful supporters and prayer partners who were there for me over the last few years.

➢ The leaders for giving me the opportunity to serve in different capacities while being aboard. I often remind myself of these words from Maya Angelou: "If you see something that you don't like, then change it. If you cannot change it, then change the way you think about it." This quote has been a significant help for me on my journey with God.

➢ All the Caribbean people who served alongside me and my prayer partners Jheanelle and Eicy

➢ Everyone who made my time aboard memorable (cabin mates—Pam and Rayyen; special friend—Julie Fast)

➢ Many of the young ladies who shared their stories with me and allowed me to speak into their lives

➢ All the children who allowed me to play with them and share in their world
➢ My wonderful ship families (Easting, Visser, and Lee)

My next step
➢ I will be leaving the ship on February 12 in Bangkok, Thailand, and will be going home to have a long vacation while I wait for the Lord to show me what is my next step and where He will lead me.

My prayer points
➢ That I will have a smooth reentry connecting with family and friends
➢ That I will continue to walk in God's perfect will for my life as He shows me the next step in His perfect timing
➢ That God will continue to supply all my needs according to His riches in glory by Christ Jesus

Thank you for partnering with me on this journey with God aboard the *Logos Hope* ship. Without your prayers and support, I could not have made it! May God continue to richly bless you! "I thank my God upon every remembrance of you" (Philippians 1:3).

In His service,
Susan Isidore

CHAPTER 5

Third Mission aboard
Logos Hope

Prophetic Word

Before leaving the ship in February 2014, God spoke into my spirit saying, "I'm not finished with you yet in this ministry. Prepare to return." These were not the words I wanted to hear; however, they were always at the back of my mind. As I settled back into life at home, more and more confirmations related to my return to the ship kept coming. After many months of internal struggles with Father God, I finally surrendered and said, "Okay, if this is Your will, then let Your will be done in my life." I did not have any further details from God about how long I would stay at home nor in what capacity I would work on the ship. I just knew I had to wait on Father God to put all the pieces together.

After one year and eight months, the puzzle started coming together after receiving a phone call from the church secretary. I was informed by the secretary that my pastor sent me an email requesting my attendance at a meeting with the OM Caribbean field leader. I quickly went to my inbox. As I started reading the letter, I sensed God saying to me, "This meeting is not just for you to represent the Woodbrook Pentecostal Church (WPC), but it is also the door for you to return to the ship."

The meeting was to discuss plans for the *Logos Hope* visit to the Caribbean in 2017. At the end of the meeting, there were further discussions with the field leader. He needed someone aboard the ship who could help with managing the onboard responsibilities for OM Caribbean during the 2017 Caribbean tour. Can you make a guess who was that person? I'm sure you guessed it right! Father God had chosen me to fill this position. He put all the pieces together and then put me in place so that everything He spoke over my life was materialized. Once again, I could attest to being excited about the plans God had for my life, even though in the beginning, it was not what I wanted.

Another Season on Board

It was now May 2016, and once more, I had to say my goodbyes. However, this time was much easier than before. In 2010, I was more apprehensive about the journey and what I would encounter. Now I was more prepared having experienced life on board the ship. I thank God for divine connections and for favor. He opened the door for me to spend the weekend in New York before traveling to Johannesburg and then on to Richards Bay, South Africa—where I met the ship. The weekend in New York was cold because it was the spring season, but I did not anticipate that South Africa would also be cold. I was not prepared for the winter season I experienced in South Africa. I did not have any winter clothing, so I had to shop for these items.

Returning to the ship this time was both exciting and different. I felt I was returning to my old residence, but a new family was now residing there. There were a few familiar faces; some were aware of my return while others were quite surprised to see me again. My new Caribbean family was very welcoming. They made me feel at home, and this was truly appreciated.

The bustle of life on the ship had begun. The morning after my arrival, the ship sailed to the next port, which was East London in South Africa. The first two nights on board, I did not get much rest because my body was still adjusting to changes in the time zone. This was further compounded by the noise which was heard from the engines during sailing. My cabin was located on deck 3, which was near the engine room. Thankfully, the third night was a little better, and I was able to get some much-needed rest.

I had one free day to adjust to life on the ship before starting work in the bookfair. This was the same department I worked in when I first joined the ship's ministry in 2010. The leadership felt the bookfair was the ideal department for me to be introduced once again to the ministry. They believed this was necessary so I could become familiar with all the new crew members. The bookfair team is the largest department on board with approximately sixty-five people.

On this occasion of rejoining the ministry, I did not have the privilege of returning to a pre-ship group. I worked with this team for a few months before I was asked to help train the new recruits in the port of Ghana. At the end of my time working in the bookfair, I was really encouraged by the notes written on my farewell card by the team members. I realized that one of the reasons God allowed me to work in the bookfair was to be a source of encouragement to the team. These members were emotionally drained from one of the earlier ports in Durban, South Africa.

I spent one month onshore in the country of Ghana before returning to the ship, at which time, I had the opportunity to work in the onboard events and help ministry departments for one month. My work with the onboard events department was very helpful. I got to experience the planning and executing of an event. I also gained a better understanding of the work done by the events team. This was also strategic as I gave suggestions that pertained to the different events expected to happen in the Caribbean countries.

The objective of working in the help ministry department was to understand its role and function and to determine how it could also be of assistance to the Caribbean islands. I thoroughly enjoyed carrying out the ground assessments for this department. These assessments were done to determine an organization's needs before any donation was given by the ship's help ministry. Being involved with these assessments allowed me the opportunity to visit different locations. The scenery en route to the various places of assessment was always breathtaking. In December 2016, after six months of being on board working in different capacities, I finally moved into my role as the onboard representative for OM Caribbean.

Memories of South Africa

Culture shock

To date, the people of South Africa are still affected by their history of apartheid. Individuals are categorized in every sphere of society into different groups such as Black South Africans,

White South Africans, Indian South Africans, and Colored South Africans who are considered people of mixed descent.

For my first five weeks of being on board the ship in South Africa, the local people had already categorized me as a Colored person. At the first two ports in South Africa, as I worked with the local people, I was asked by some of them if I was from South Africa. When I indicated to them that I am from Trinidad and Tobago in the Caribbean, they responded by saying, "You could pass as a Colored person here in South Africa because you will fit into this group."

This question was most likely posed to me because of my lighter skin complexion. I am from a mixed background of African, French, and Spanish. The frequency of this question made me feel a bit uncomfortable. I have never experienced anything like this in my home country Trinidad and Tobago. We are a cosmopolitan nation, and people have accepted this fact, so a person's ethnicity is rarely talked about. I see the continual categorization of people in the world as a plan of the enemy. This plan of the enemy is to keep people in bondage by reminding them of the past. The past of apartheid, slavery, and colonialism, to name a few, are all very difficult events in history the enemy uses to keep segregation alive. The sad fact about all of this is that segregation can still be found in certain parts of South Africa. Thankfully, God uses the *Logos Hope* ministry to show that people from many nations can come together as one, all to spread the good news of Jesus Christ.

This has been a huge blessing and testimony to many nations across the world. This testimony is an example of unity as it shows people from fifty-five to sixty different countries working and living together as a big family on board a ship. I am grateful to God for having allowed me to be a part of this ministry and to experience what He is doing in and around the world.

Historical milestones

The *Logos Hope* made history during its visit to South Africa. Since she started sailing in 2009, this was her first voyage to South Africa crossing over the Indian Ocean into the Atlantic Ocean. The voyage was a bit rough at the beginning, but by the second day, the seas were much calmer. As we sailed into Cape Town, we were greeted with a warm welcome from many visitors on the quay side. A local helicopter flew overhead to take the perfect picture of the ship along with her crew members waving their national flags. The view while sailing into the port was quite breathtaking. It was a great display of the greatness and beauty of God's creation.

There was another significant moment for *Logos Hope*, which occurred when we arrived at the port in Cape Town, South Africa. The twenty-year-old computer system in the bookfair was replaced with a new one. While on board during my first term, I worked with the old system. There were plans to change the old computer system on numerous occasions, but because of several challenges, the change had to be deferred.

The bookfair and ICT teams were quite busy during the installation of the new system. As usual, the familiarization of any new system would experience certain teething problems. Nevertheless, with time, everyone became familiar with the new system. It was a great privilege for me to experience this significant moment given the fact that I worked with the old system, and now I was a part of the first team to use the new system.

Caribbean Visit—Part 1

Having spent one year visiting certain countries in the Caribbean region, I was asked by some persons, "Which is your favorite Caribbean country?" My response would usually be, "I really don't have an answer to this question. I thoroughly enjoyed experiencing the uniqueness of all the countries, and I appreciated seeing God's beauty in each island." As we sailed around the Caribbean, it was a little difficult not to compare Trinidad and Tobago with other islands. However, this experience made me even more appreciative of what we have on our twin islands. The goal of *the Logos Hope's* visit to the Caribbean was to bring *Hope* from shore to shore. We were engaged in recruiting and mobilizing people to pray, give, and go: *Pray* for missions and missionaries, give toward missions and missionaries, and *go* into missions.

Guyana

Our first port on this tour was Guyana. Geographically, this country is not part of the Caribbean region; however, linguistically, historically, and demographically, it is considered part of the Caribbean. It also forms part of the Caribbean Community (CARICOM). In this port, our Caribbean team had the responsibility of setting up the OM Caribbean connect area on deck 4. This connect area was nicely located in one corner of the deck, which was cordoned off from the rest of the International Café.

At the front of the connecting area, there was a lovely banner that displayed the mission and vision of OM Caribbean. On the back wall of the sitting area, there was a large world map, which persons could see from afar. On another part of the wall, there was a nice display of stories from some of the Caribbean missionaries. There were also different types of literature for distribution. Finally, there were two round tables with a seating capacity of two people at each table.

This arrangement was in preparation for discussions on missions, prayer requests, counseling, or any other need the Holy Spirit would facilitate through the OM Caribbean team members. We anticipated many visitors from each country in the region. Nevertheless, the ministry in the port of Guyana was not very busy, but there were some good connections with the local people at the round tables. During this time, the ship's community also enjoyed the 2016 Christmas season and New Year celebrations for 2017.

Trinidad and Tobago

From Guyana, the tour continued firstly to Trinidad and then to Tobago, where *Logos Hope* is known as "the book ship." Since her previous visit in 2009, people had been eagerly awaiting her return. When the ship sailed into the beautiful waters of Trinidad, my heart became filled with pride and joy as I saw my homeland. Not many crew members get to experience this unique occasion of sailing into their country.

In the port of Trinidad, we welcomed over ninety thousand visitors on the ship in just over three-weeks. During that time, while *Logos Hope* was busy welcoming many visitors, seventy-five new recruits from around the world were engaged in their pre-ship and basic safety training at the Victory Heights retreat facility. After their training, the group sailed to Tobago on the interisland ferry called the T&T Spirit, where they became part of the *Logos Hope* crew known as pre-ship training (PST) Port of Spain. This port was quite intense for all the Trinbagonians. However, we all enjoyed the opportunity to host loved ones on board our floating home, as well as visit with family and friends on shore. It was a pleasant experience to see the night view from Port of Spain and its environs as we left the shores of Trinidad.

We sailed overnight to Tobago and arrived at 8:00 a.m. the next day. The Port of Scarborough was not as busy as the Port of Spain. However, some people who did not get the opportunity to visit the ship in Trinidad traveled to Tobago to experience the ship's ministry. The crew members thoroughly enjoyed the beaches in the beautiful isle of Tobago. Many of them traveled around the island, sightseeing on their days off, and participated in evangelism programs and faith trips.

A faith trip can be defined as a trip taken by faith. Most times, a small group of persons would leave the ship for one day to fulfill certain assignments while connecting with the local people. These crew members would have little or no money and would have to put their faith and trust in God to provide all that is needed for the day such as food and transportation.

When our time in Trinidad and Tobago came to an end, it was a great relief mixed with excitement—a great relief from all the demands of a busy port and excitement hearing all the positive feedback about the ship's visit. Fellow crew members expressed to us Trinbagonians how much they loved our beautiful country as well as the kindness and hospitality of its people.

ABC islands

After spending over five weeks in Trinidad and Tobago, we had the opportunity to experience the beautiful ABC islands which are Aruba, Bonaire, and Curaçao. These islands share a Dutch colonial history and West Indian heritage. Most people on the islands speak a minimum of four languages: Papiamentu, Dutch, English, and Spanish. It is quite interesting to note that each island has a unique twist on the Papiamentu language, which is a mixture of Portuguese, English, Spanish, and French.

In the country of Curaçao, many of the ship's onshore outreaches and onboard events focused on sharing hope with people trapped in difficult situations. One of the special events was geared toward ladies who work in the red-light district—a concentration of prostitution and sex-oriented businesses. Many women travel to Curaçao on special visas to work for the legal brothels located around the island.

In this port, I enjoyed working with and getting to know all the people in the Operation Mobilization (OM) Caribbean working group. In Curaçao, OM does not have an office or a base with a field leader, but instead, several people work together as a group. The members of the group did an excellent job of being my host, especially during the one-month dry dock period. During this time, I worked at the base camp, which was located at the Isla Refinery in Curaçao. I was a part of the support team that helped with the logistics and member care for the land-based (challenge) teams as well as the families. I also assisted the training team, where I taught some sessions on basic leadership training for crew members.

At the end of the dry dock period, the governor of Curaçao invited some members of the ship's community to a special "thank-you" reception at her palace. This event was thoroughly enjoyed by everyone who attended. The lovely evening was filled with fun, food, and fellowship and was seen as a blessing and reward from God for all the hard work that was done during the month.

At the end of my two-year commitment on board, I had the opportunity to return to Curaçao for a one-month vacation. Once again, because of God's divine connections, I was able to stay at the residence of a member of the OM Caribbean working group. Angèle was a great host as she welcomed me into her home and made me a part of her family for that month. For the first week, I was able to have time for relaxation. In the second week, I began to explore other parts of the island that I did not experience when I lived aboard the ship. It was also great to reconnect with some of the other members of the working group.

Bonaire was the second port of call in the Dutch ABC islands and has a population of less than twenty thousand permanent inhabitants. Our visit to this island was very short, and during this time, we celebrated Easter weekend. On deck 4, we were able to encourage local believers in their faith; however, not many people were interested in joining the ministry. There is no university or college in Bonaire, and most teenagers leave the island after high school. They usually visit Holland or Curaçao where they would complete their studies. Most of them stay in these countries for better opportunities.

In the port of Bonaire, we were able to see favorable results from our recruitment drive, which was done in the first four ports of the Caribbean tour. Three people from the Caribbean joined the ship in the Short-Term Exposure Program (STEP). We welcomed to the ship a young man and a young lady from Trinidad and one lady from Guyana. We were thankful to God that people were responding positively to the call of missions. During this port, I felt a little exhausted. I had limited time to prepare for the new port, and my body was still recovering from the demanding dry dock schedule.

After our short stay in Bonaire, we had a smooth three-day sail to Aruba. This is the most developed of the islands, with golf courses, malls, and many casinos and international restaurants in the capital Oranjestad. One of the first things that caught my attention as we arrived in Aruba was the beautifully painted vehicles carrying tourists and playing loud calypso music.

It was a very busy period for me at the beginning of this port. OM Caribbean had a meeting aboard the ship, and I was responsible for hosting all the board members. It was also a busy time for our connect area on deck 4 as there were many people interested in getting into missions and enquiring about joining the ship's ministry. For my ministry day, I had the opportunity to visit a Spanish-speaking church. In Aruba, there are several Spanish-speaking churches because there are many people from Colombia, Dominican Republic, and Venezuela.

Jeremiah 33:3 (KJV) says, "Call upon me, and I will answer you, and show you great and mighty things, which you know not." In the previous Port of Bonaire when I told Father God I was exhausted, I did not know He had already put things in place for me to get a vacation. He graciously provided accommodation at the home of one of the board members, in the person of Pastor Cedric Charles and his lovely wife, Mrs. Suzette Charles. This beautiful couple was the perfect host, as they cared for me like their own daughter. I was grateful to Father God for His favor as I was able to rest and be refreshed for five days before continuing my journey with the ship.

Jamaica

The Caribbean tour continued, as we sailed to the country of Jamaica to the first port in Kingston. In March 2010, I had the opportunity to visit Kingston for five days as part of my pretraining with OM Caribbean. Little did I know that seven years later, I would be back aboard *Logos Hope* as part of the crew, sailing into Kingston to share knowledge, help, and hope with the people of Jamaica. This was an extremely busy port for everyone aboard.

There was a lot of rain for the first few days in the port, and this hindered the people from visiting the ship. In the third week, the rain ceased, and the people came out in their numbers. On some days, visitors would stand in long lines for more than two hours; however, they were still excited to come aboard and purchase the famous King James Bible among many other books. *Logos Hope* welcomed over 117,000 visitors during the first five weeks in the Port of Kingston.

In this port, we enjoyed a special ministry by Babbie Mason, who is an American gospel singer and songwriter. Two of her famous songs are "Standing in the Gap for You" and "Trust His Heart." It was a privilege to host Babbie and her husband and to be the mistress of ceremonies (MC) at her ladies' event. The ship also hosted the Global Missions Orientation (GMO) training aboard. The attendants were mainly from Trinidad and Tobago, Curaçao, and Aruba, and these were direct fruits of the recruiting drive. Most of the participants became interested in missions because of the ship's visit to their country within the first few months of the Caribbean tour.

In each port, the partner ministry division would recruit several port volunteers to help with the workload aboard the ship. In some countries, the volunteers also assist with translation. Part of my responsibility as the OM Caribbean representative was to welcome these port volunteers to the ship's ministry. I also gave training sessions about OM Caribbean, and prior to leaving the port, we had a farewell event where I thanked them for their work and service.

It was always a joy to listen to some of their testimonies about their experiences aboard, especially the different lessons they learned from God. One of the volunteers named Charles shared an experience he had with the Lord. While working in the International Café, one of his duties was to continually sweep popcorn off the floor. During this time, God started speaking to him concerning his marriage. God said, "Just as you are serving the visitors by continually cleaning the floor, so too, you need to continually be patient in serving your wife." Charles stated that this lesson helped restore his marriage. As he was pondering on what God was teaching him, he then asked God, "Why did marriages from the past last longer than present marriages?" God said to him, "In the past, people made their vows to Me, and they honored it, but now, people are making vows to each other and are dishonoring it." I believe this lesson was very profound, and we could all learn from it.

After our time in Kingston, we sailed overnight to the Port of Montego Bay. This berth was much more scenic than the Coal berth in Kingston. Montego Bay is known as a tourist destination. This port was very busy with visits from several cruise ships. As a result, the *Logos Hope* had to share the port with these ships; and on certain days, the bookfair only opened during the evening time. However, on some days, we were able to accommodate a few school visits during the morning period. All in all, our time in Jamaica was very busy but enjoyable. Many people showed great interest in learning more about the ministry, and some even showed potential for being a part of missions.

Emergency Trip to Trinidad

Psalm 37:23 (KJV) says, "The steps of a good man are ordered by the LORD: and he delights in his way," and Jeremiah 29:11 says, "For I know the plans I have for you declares the Lord plans to prosper you and not to harm you, plans to give you hope and a future."

Based on my life's events in May and June, I can truly say without a shadow of a doubt that God orders our steps as we submit to His will and His ways. All of this in an effort to bring fulfillment to His purpose in our lives.

Two weeks before returning to Trinidad, I became very tired emotionally, mentally, and spiritually. This was because of the difficulties experienced in the Port of Kingston, along with the general demands of life on board the ship. This tiredness affected my prayer life, and I was unable to wake up to pray during the early hours of the morning. This was the time the Holy Spirit would usually nudge me to pray. However, on the afternoon of Friday, June 30, I felt the need to visit deck 7 to be refreshed. As I was there, simply observing the beautiful scenery in the Port of Montego Bay, I started talking to Daddy God. My speech then turned into worship, and I began singing a song that came from the book of Psalm. "I will lift up my eyes unto the hills from whence cometh my help, my help cometh from the Lord which made heaven and earth" (Psalm 121:1–2 KJV).

As I continued making this declaration, my spirit started to soar, and I felt strengthened. I left the deck, feeling encouraged, not knowing that I would need strength the next morning as the Holy Spirit woke me up to pray. Unknown to me, this prayer time in Jamaica turned out to be a period of intercession for my mom who fell ill during this exact time back in Trinidad.

Later on in the morning, I received a call from my brother who informed me that my mom was in the hospital because she suffered a stroke the night before. I got this news just as I was preparing to help facilitate an HIV/AIDS training workshop. I then informed the team leader about my current situation and was released from my duties that morning. After receiving this news, I immediately prayed and asked God what was His will for me in this situation. I sensed that God wanted me to travel home to be with my mother and brother during that time. Even though the circumstances of my leaving the ship were not ideal, God, in His wisdom, saw fit to remove me from the ship at this time. I believe if I had continued the journey at that time, I would have gotten burned out.

I left for Trinidad on the morning of July 3, and *Logos Hope* sailed out of Montego Bay later that day to make her way to Nassau, Bahamas. I visited my mom in the hospital the day after my arrival in Trinidad, and she was released into my care. I thanked God that I could be home to care for her with the help of my aunty Marcia and my brother Shaun. I am particularly grateful that God spared her life so that I could pray with her during that time and encourage her to rededicate her life to Jesus. I also reminded her about the importance of committing her life to Jesus's care and truly living for God.

Besides caring for my mom, I also got some much-needed rest and thoroughly enjoyed being able to eat home-cooked food. I spent three weeks at home and felt refreshed after having fellowship at my local church and being able to connect briefly with some family and friends. Everyone was very supportive during this time. Yet again, I am grateful to God and can testify that my mother has made a full recovery and has returned to her normal way of life. All praise, glory, and honor belong to a faithful God.

Caribbean Visit—Part 2

Bahamas

I rejoined the crew on July 23 and got to experience four days of the Bahamian culture in Nassau. The Bahamas consists of seven-hundred-plus islands, some of which are uninhabited, and others are filled with beautiful resorts.

After *Logos Hope*'s three-week stay in Nassau, we sailed overnight to Freeport, one of the other islands. This island experienced extensive damage from a tropical storm in 2015, and many of the churches are still in the rebuilding process. This was *Logos Hope*'s first visit to Freeport; however, her sister ship *Logos II* visited the island in 2008. In this port, there were not many visitors as this area was not central to many of the activities on the island, and local transportation was not available on that particular route.

I thank God for the continued divine appointments even in the ports where I least expected them. In the first week, I had the opportunity to meet with one of the local doctors and his wife when they visited the ship. Dr. Collie was originally from Nassau but moved to Freeport ten years prior to working in the medical field. He was elated when he met me and discovered that I was from Trinidad. He has a great love for Trinidad because he pursued his medical studies there. He also had the opportunity to visit Faith Revival Ministry headed by the late apostle Bertril Baird. Dr. Collie also visited my home church, Woodbrook Pentecostal Church (WPC), which at that time was headed by the late apostle Joshua Turnel Nelson. He further shared that he was tremendously blessed for having known these two men of God.

These men of God were also dear to me because they were my spiritual fathers in the faith. Dr. Collie is also the pastor of a small church in Freeport, and he extended an invitation for me to visit his church along with a team from the ship. Included in this invitation was also the opportunity to preach the Word of God.

Haiti

After a three-day sail from the Bahamas, we entered the country Haiti. For thirty years, there was no ship ministry to Haiti. However, in August 2017, *Logos Hope* changed the statistics as she was docked at Port-au-Prince, the capital and largest city in the country. We all enjoyed the beautiful scenery as we sailed into the port. However, through our spiritual eyes, we were able to sense the heaviness and feel the spiritual dryness in the atmosphere.

Prior to our arrival in this country, crew members were encouraged to pray fervently because of the intensity of the spiritual warfare in this nation. Our time in Haiti was very intense, and there were many restrictions because of the security issues within the country. We were not allowed to be outside the ship after 5:00 p.m. and were only allowed to go out in groups of three with a local person who had their own vehicle. The ship was closed to the public at 5:00 p.m., and all local port volunteers had to disembark the ship at the same time.

Crew members were busy during the daytime as they were involved in a number of orphanage visits and practical work. These projects were organized by OM Caribbean and OM Haiti. There are a number of orphanages in Haiti, resulting from a lack of education and poverty, which has a great effect on family life. Many children have been abandoned because of unwanted pregnancies by young girls.

On deck 4, the OM Caribbean team was extremely busy as many people were asking how they could become a volunteer aboard the ship. Most of these people were not necessarily interested in getting involved in missions, but they were looking for a way to escape to leave their country. We had to continually remind them that we are all missionaries and did not receive an income. However, some people were genuinely interested in the ministry. We prayed that some of them would join the OM Haiti office to support the local pastor who works there.

During our two-and-a-half-week stay in Haiti, I left the ship on two occasions: the first was to visit a local supermarket, and the second was a visit to a local church. This church was greatly affected by the earthquake in 2010 but was able to rebuild part of the structure. During our visit to the church, one of the members shared his testimony with us. He stated that during the 2010 earthquake, his wife was in labor, and he could not get to the hospital because all the roads were blocked.

As he looked outside, he saw a team of doctors passing by his home, so he went and shared with them what was happening with his wife. Two of these medical doctors stayed at his home for two days to help deliver his baby girl. When she was born, he made a vow to God that he will never stop singing praises to Him. He told God that the child would also sing unto Him. To date, the family of four sings songs of worship in their church services and also in other meeting places.

Dominican Republic

From Haiti, the ship sailed to Jamaica for a one-day technical stop to receive fuel. After this, we sailed to the Dominican Republic (DR), which shares the island of Hispaniola with Haiti on the west side. We spent one month in this country, and there, we said goodbye to crew members who ended their commitment. We also welcomed one hundred new crew members aboard. In this group, we had the great opportunity to welcome twelve recruits from the Caribbean—representatives from Trinidad and Tobago, Curaçao, Aruba, and Jamaica. This number represented some of the fruits of our recruitment drive earlier that year.

In 2017, the Caribbean region experienced a very active hurricane season. There were two devastating hurricanes during this time—Irma and Maria. They both threatened the island of Hispaniola while the ship was there. On both occasions, the captain and his team sailed the ship out into the southern part of the ocean to seek safety for the crew and the vessel. The unexpected voyages meant that several events and onshore outreaches had to be canceled. Thankfully, most of them were rescheduled for later dates. Our time at sea was spent praying for the affected Caribbean islands and for crew members who were seasick. The ship was berthed in the Port of Santo Domingo, which is the capital of the Dominican Republic. This area was not damaged by the hurricanes, so we were able to complete the visit.

Despite having to leave the port on two occasions, we were still able to receive over forty-eight thousand visitors. Added to this, a number of people were interested in being part of the ministry. We thanked God for His mercies and protection in keeping us safe and for the many people across the globe who prayed for us during this time.

Saint Kitts

The ship continued its Caribbean tour of bringing hope from shore to shore as we sailed into the beautiful island of Saint Kitts. The Federation of Saint Kitts and Nevis is the smallest sovereign state in the western hemisphere in both area and population. This was a short, four-day visit, but we made the most of our time there. Almost nineteen thousand people visited the ship, and many of them had been longing for her return since the last visit seven years prior.

I had the opportunity to visit one church whose pastor was originally from Tobago, and I also got to reconnect with my cousin, who now resides in Nevis with her family. Some of the crew received a government-sponsored train tour, which enabled us to see part of the island and learn more about its history.

Antigua and Barbuda

The ship's planned visit to Antigua was "up in the air" when we heard of the hurricanes being directed straight toward the islands. We were saddened to hear of the devastation to the island of Barbuda and were grateful to God that we could still visit Antigua, as they were not directly affected.

The initial plan was for a *Logos Hope* team to visit Barbuda for one week. However, because of the devastation in Barbuda, many of the residents moved to Antigua, which made it possible for them to visit the ship. We hosted a few events aboard the ship to encourage the residents of Barbuda to keep trusting God in the midst of trials. *Logos Hope* is not equipped as a disaster relief vessel, but we were delighted that we could partner with Samaritan's Purse. This is an International Christian Relief organization, which has been working on the islands after the hurricanes.

For a duration of the two weeks in Antigua, *Logos Hope* teams flew over to Barbuda every morning with Samaritan's Purse. These teams assisted with some of the cleanup and restorative work on the island. *Logos Hope* continued with her help ministry's initiatives to the island of Dominica. A donation was made toward relief work that was being done on the island. Dominica was greatly affected by one of the major hurricanes that season.

In this port of Antigua, I had the privilege of connecting with Rev. Nigel Henry, who at that time was the missions director of the Pentecostal Assemblies of the West Indies World Mission Agency (PAWIWMA). He is also the pastor of a church in Barbuda that was affected during the hurricane. Pastor Henry and his members were now congregating at a temporary location in Antigua. There, they facilitated a team from *Logos Hope* that took charge of the main service.

Over the years, PAWIWMA solicited prayers from the different PAWI churches for the missionaries that were on the field. In Trinidad, my home church is part of the Pentecostal Assemblies of the West Indies (PAWI). I was given the opportunity to personally thank the congregation for their prayer and support and also shared a few testimonies about my mission experiences. Our team encouraged the church members to continue trusting God despite their current situation. It was nice meeting with Mrs. Henry, who said to me, "I have been praying for you for many years, and now I am happy to see you in person."

During this time, I also connected with Rev. Pat Glasgow, the then–general bishop of PAWI, as both he and Rev. Nigel Henry treated me to a lovely meal and took me sightseeing on the island. The ship's community had a good time in Antigua. We were able to challenge the young people to live for Jesus and to trust Him in their desire to step out into missions.

Saint Lucia

From Antigua, we sailed overnight to another beautiful island, Saint Lucia. All of these islands in the Eastern Caribbean region are well-known to foreigners as they are considered tourist destinations. In this country, we were only planning to visit the Port of Castries for three weeks. However, in the second week of our stay in the port, a cruise ship arrived, so the *Logos* ship had to leave the berth. The ship had to anchor out in the ocean for seven days or plan a spontaneous trip to the southern side of the island in Vieux Fort. We chose the latter option. I was excited to visit Saint Lucia after hearing so much about this beautiful island. I was also thrilled to connect with some of my former colleagues from Bible school who reside there. It was a great pleasure to reconnect with each one of them as we shared stories about our life and ministry since graduating from Bible school.

One of my ministry days in Castries was spent helping to lead a prayer station in the city area, with a team from Youth with a Mission (YWAM). It was a great experience to meet with people and ask them, "How can I pray for you?" This was the first time I saw this type of ministry in action. I prayed for some of the young people who were hanging out "liming" at the end of their school day.

During our brief time at the end of the meeting, the YWAM leader asked me, "What is your full name?" I answered her question, and then she said, "Your face looks familiar. Are you the PAWI missionary?"

I smiled and said, "I am from a PAWI church."

She then replied, "We have been praying for you, and it's so nice to meet up with you."

They then invited me out to have a meal to show appreciation for my work and service to the Lord. I thank God for all the people who have been praying for me over the years, especially those I have not been aware.

The time spent in Vieux Fort was short, but we still had several visitors, especially the school children who were excited to visit the ship. A team of us visited the Vieux Fort library where the ship donated books. There, we had the opportunity to do a presentation for the young children in the community.

On one particular Sunday, I visited a local church. This day happened to be the same day on which "Creole Day" was celebrated in Saint Lucia. I shared with the congregation that my hometown in Paramin, Trinidad, also acknowledges and celebrates this special day. Some of the older people in Paramin speak French creole also known as "patois," which is the second language in Saint Lucia.

Barbados

The Caribbean tour continued as we left Saint Lucia and sailed to the beautiful isle of Barbados. This was another busy port aboard the ship. During that time, there were several onboard guests because of OM board meetings being hosted. After several months, it was good to reconnect with some of the

OM Caribbean board members. However, my immediate boss, the then OM Caribbean field leader Henry Janowski, fell ill. He was unable to visit the ship as had been scheduled. Sadly, a few months later, he went home to glory to be with the Lord.

I met Henry for the first time in 2010 during my initial OM Caribbean pretraining and thereafter connected with him whenever he made visits to the ship as the OM Caribbean field leader. I am grateful to God for allowing me to serve with him for ten months during the Caribbean tour. It was a pleasure to know him. I know his legacy will live on for the work that he did within the OM Caribbean field.

In this port, I also visited one of the local churches. On my day off, I was treated to a nice outing by a friend whom I met seven years prior at my OM Caribbean pretraining. Similar to Saint Lucia, this port was very hectic because of the busy cruise ship season. Again, the *Logos Hope* ship had to leave the berth a few days earlier to go out to anchor. Despite these changes, we were able to welcome over thirty thousand visitors aboard. Several people asked the question, "Why did the ship take so long before returning to the Caribbean?" We had to explain that the organization has one ship that served the eastern part of the world after leaving the Caribbean in 2010. We were thankful to God for all the people who expressed interest in joining the ministry, and we looked forward to seeing them serve in the mission field in the near future.

Saint Vincent and the Grenadines

Logos Hope continued her tour of sharing knowledge, help, and hope with the people of the Caribbean. Our next port of call was Kingstown in Saint Vincent and the Grenadines, where the ship was berthed for two weeks in the center of the city. The capital city of Kingstown is known to have at least four hundred arches and is also referred to as the city of arches. Once more, I had the opportunity to preach at one of the member churches of the Pentecostal Assemblies of the West Indies (PAWI). I also reconnected with friends whom I knew from Bible school. It was also a great pleasure to visit my friend Cherish and stay at her home overnight. It was nice to be off the ship for one night. We enjoyed each other's company as she took me around the island the following day, where I was able to visit the botanical garden which is part of the oldest forest reserve in the West. I also visited the beach location where they filmed the movie *Pirates of the Caribbean*. I met Cherish a few years prior when she spent three months on board the *Logos Hope* in the Short-Term Exposure Program (STEP). At that time, I had the privilege to be her mentor.

Grenada

As the last month in the year 2017 approached, so too did the last port in the Caribbean visit which was Saint Georges, Grenada. This was a very short port as we were only opened to the public for six days to facilitate the transitional period aboard. The ship transitioned from the Caribbean region to the Latin American region where she was expected to spend two and a half years.

At the bookfair, 70 percent of the English books were removed and replaced with Spanish books. While all of this was happening on board, a few teams from the ship set up shops in five different locations around the island of Grenada. There was a branch of *Logos Hope*'s bookfair near almost everyone in Grenada. Yet again, I had the opportunity to reconnect with two of my former classmates from Bible school who I had not seen in years. They were very hospitable, and they took me around the island. I was able to explore one of the forts, the beautiful ocean, the lush mountainous areas, and some of their natural wonders.

The Caribbean tour came to an end with an evaluation meeting that assessed the outcome of the ship's visit to the region. At this meeting, there were representatives from the onshore leadership team, the onboard leadership team, and three representatives from OM Caribbean which included me. During the meeting, I was asked the question, "What was a highlight for you while working with OM Caribbean for the last year?"

My response was as follows:

> *The last twelve months have been one of great divine connections and networking. The Lord has placed me in a strategic position to form relationships within the Caribbean region for future ministry opportunities. It was also a time of stretching but very fulfilling and rewarding, as I saw the fruits of my labor in recruiting and mobilizing people on deck 4 to go into missions. It gave me great pleasure to serve aboard Logos Hope, alongside some of the said people that were encouraged by the OM Caribbean team to step out in faith and trust God to go out into missions. I continued to say that I am happy to be a part of what God is doing in the bigger work of missions, especially as it relates to the Caribbean region. Another big highlight for me was seeing my former classmates from Bible school in positions of influence, fulfilling their God-given purpose.*

My last assignment with the OM Caribbean team was to coordinate with Caribbean crew members in planning a "Celebration of the Caribbean" segment. This was part of the last prayer night for the region. It entailed worship and giving thanks to God for all the work that was done in the Caribbean. The group of Caribbean crew members did an amazing job in preparing some of the famous delicacies from each island. I thoroughly enjoyed working together with the team.

During the Caribbean tour of 2017, I had great pleasure working together with and getting to know the various OM Caribbean teams. It was also very eventful working with all the Caribbean crew members, especially the new recruits who were mobilized during our tour. I give God thanks for all that was accomplished throughout the year and for all the fruits that are yet to be birthed from this tour.

Ministry in Trinidad and Tobago

My ministry opportunities in this port started while we were sailing into the waters of Trinidad. It is a custom on the ship as we sail into a new country that we meet for prayer and worship early in the morning on the bow. Sailing into Trinidad was no different. However, on this occasion, the flow of worship and prayer was a bit difficult because the atmosphere was very heavy.

At the beginning of the session, I noticed a dark cloud hovering over the sunrise. As we continued in prayer, I felt the Spirit of the Lord saying to me, "You need to pray specifically for this dark cloud that is over your nation. The sunrise represents My presence that is in Trinidad, but the dark cloud represents the darkness that is hovering over your land, and it is hindering My presence." I shared this revelation with the group and encouraged everyone to pray in this regard. As we prayed and took authority over the atmosphere, the sunlight pierced through the cloud, and the skies became very bright. Everyone on the bow felt the difference, and we were then able to freely worship God without any more hindrances in the atmosphere.

I also had the opportunity to have my first interview at a television station. A team of three crew members including myself did an interview at the Trinity Communications Network station. We shared about *Logos Hope*'s visit to Trinidad and Tobago as well as a short testimony about ministry involvement on board.

During my time in Tobago, God provided me with some great connections, and He also moved mightily on one of my ministry days. It all started at the beginning of the port when a local Christian bookseller came on board. While setting up his book table at the front entrance of the ship, I walked past his table and greeted him. He then asked, "Are you a television or radio host?"

I said, "No, sir."

He then gave me a prophetic word, saying, "God will use your voice in the media, and He will allow you to speak to many nations. Your voice is very soothing and will demand attention because of the anointing on your life, and God has also gifted you for this."

On that same day, I had two persons come up to me on different occasions and said, "I heard your voice even before I saw you." I took this as confirmation of what God said to me earlier that day about Him allowing my voice to be distinct.

Another ministry opportunity was at a prayer and worship program named "Outpouring." At this meeting, we had a powerful time of prayer and worship with the outpouring of God's presence. Toward the end of the program, God used me to bring forth a prophetic word for the church, where I shared that "God wants the church to arise to pray for our nation." At the end of the program, we were informed that the session was videotaped and would be broadcasted on a local television station in Tobago. We were all surprised because we were unaware that our ministry day was going to be televised.

In each port, the ship has an "official opening and a thank-you" reception. The official opening is a time when the ship's team would invite special guests, including a guest of honor from the host country. This individual would officially declare the opening of the *Logos Hope* bookfair to the public. The "thank-you" reception was held at the end of the visit where the ship's team would thank all the official sponsors and others for having made the ship's visit possible.

During the "thank-you" reception in Tobago, I met two beautiful ladies whom I connected with really well. As I was speaking with one of these ladies whose name is Marva, she told me that God showed her a title for one of the books I would write. The name God showed her was "While You Wait." I thanked her for her word of knowledge, and then I said to her, "I am aware that God wants me to write about my story, and I would take note of the title." Later that night, I made a journal entry about this divine appointment and also documented the title that God gave for my book. After this meeting with Marva, I waited for the time and season to begin writing.

God is faithful, and He is always speaking. We just need to be sensitive to the Holy Spirit and what He is saying to us. We also need to know the right time when we must act upon what the Holy Spirit has said to us. I give God praise and thanks for choosing to use me as a mouthpiece for His honor and glory and for using different people to speak into my life. These prophetic words were confirmation of what God had already spoken to me by His Holy Spirit.

Gifts and Talents

I knew you before I formed you in your mother's womb. Before you were born I set you apart and appointed you as my prophet to the nations.

—Jeremiah 1:5

God has designed each human being uniquely and has placed gifts and talents within this individual to complement his or her personality. All of this is to aid in fulfilling one's God-given purpose. Apart from our natural gifts and talents, God has also blessed us with spiritual gifts. These gifts are only materialized after our spirit is regenerated when we enter into a personal relationship with God through His Son, Jesus Christ.

During the many years of waiting on God, my spiritual gifts were identified and developed as I was given opportunities to utilize them. Proverbs 18:16 (KJV) says, "A man's gift makes room for him and brings him before great men." I am thankful to God for the gifts and talents He has given me, especially in the area of teaching. I love empowering people, and this gift of teaching allows me to do this through training others and preaching.

Upon my return to the ship on this last occasion, I was afforded more opportunities to help with the onboard training of crew members, as well as sharing the Word of God in various events. There were also opportunities for me to assist people with English because many nationalities spoke English as a second language. I was privileged to be the main speaker for a "Women of Faith" event in the country of Namibia, which had about three-hundred-plus attendees. My message described a woman of faith as being one who has learned to completely trust and fear God through obedience and submission to His

Word and will. Many days after the event, people were still talking about the positive impact the message had on the ladies who were present.

Another great opportunity to minister the Word of God was in a local church in the Bahamas. I never imagined sharing in the Bahamas, especially at a church where my spiritual father, the late apostle Bertril Baird, preached a few years prior. My last preaching engagement was in the country of Mexico, where I ministered three times one morning during the church's three services. Some of the other countries I ministered in while on the ship were Gabon, Cameroon, Saint Vincent, and Colombia. I will forever be grateful to God for choosing me to help empower others across the globe and for the encouraging feedback I received after the messages were delivered.

Another spiritual gift I received is in the area of the apostolic. This has enabled me to do pioneering work both on and off the field. One of the signs of the apostle is patience, which is part of the fruit of the spirit and this has been developed in my life over the many years of waiting during different seasons. "Truly the signs of an apostle were wrought among you in all patience, in signs, and wonders, and mighty deeds" (2 Corinthians 12:12 KJV). I could remember one of my friends jokingly said to me, "At the end of all of those years of waiting on God, you will have more patients than a hospital."

Even before going into the missions field, God opened doors and placed me in unique positions. Some of these roles were very challenging because I had to create brand-new ideas for the position. After building a foundation for the position, I would then train someone to be my successor. The role I occupied as the OM Caribbean onboard representative was no different. I had to discover certain aspects of the work and put systems in place to obtain the objectives that were set out by the field leader. As different teams came aboard to work together with me, learning occurred as we went along the journey. The highlight of learning all of this new information made things easier for the crew member from OM Latin America, who worked in this capacity after my departure. She benefited from all the notes along with the experiences I shared with her about my journey throughout the year in the Caribbean.

God did not stop there; during the last four months of service on board, He created another new position for me to pioneer. I worked as the personal administrator for the hotel and catering division. In this capacity, I had the responsibility to assist the three managers and the director in bringing greater cohesion to the administrative work within their departments. After setting up the position and putting various systems in place, I then trained a young lady who succeeded me.

Prior to working as a personal administrator, the new apprentice had no administrative experience but functioned well because of the systems that were put in place for her. God is so faithful. This young lady excelled greatly in the position, so much so that almost one year after, she informed me that she was assigned to be the personal assistant to the managing director of the ship. This was also a position in which I worked a few years prior.

Once again, I had a grateful heart toward God for allowing me to empower others and see them excel in their areas of work and service. There is a great feeling of fulfillment one can experience as he or she helps to empower others.

Farewell Testimony

Isaiah 46:9–10 (KJV) says, "Remember the former things of old, For I am God, and there is no other; I am God, and there is none like Me, declaring the end from the beginning, and from ancient times things that are not yet done, saying, 'My counsel shall stand, and I will do all My pleasure."

God Almighty has spoken everything into being, including the beginning and the ending of our seasons as we submit to His plans and purpose for our lives. Two months before my second departure from *Logos Hope*, I pondered whether or not I should share my testimony. Four years prior, at the end of my first tour with the ship, I shared my testimony, and because of this, I felt there was no need to share a second one.

One morning during my quiet time as I continued pondering on this thought, I felt God saying to me, "This testimony is not about you, but it's about giving Me the glory for what I have done in and through your life." He then started downloading into my spirit what I should write. I thanked God for reminding me that I was created for His pleasure to bring glory to Him through my life. "For God is working in you, giving you the desire and the power to do what pleases Him" (Philippians 2:13).

I now give you the opportunity to read my second testimony about my time aboard *Logos Hope*.

> Dear supporters/prayer partners,
>
> "I have fought a good fight, I have finished my course, I have kept the faith" (2 Timothy 4:7 KJV).
>
> It is time once again for me to say, "So long, farewell," to this unique family and ministry called *Logos Hope*. It has been quite an interesting journey for me on board this ship. After hearing about "how to share our story" during morning devotions on January 4, 2018, I found myself having one of those heart conversations with Daddy God. I asked

Him, "What is the real reason You brought me to *Logos Hope* [my story]?" I knew some of the reasons but still couldn't grasp the real purpose.

During prayer night later that evening, journalist Julie Knox started sharing about the amazing history of the original ship. This was also the anniversary date of the shipwreck for that original ship called *Logos*. Julie continued sharing about the ministry's impact which affected many people and generations. I felt the Lord saying to me, *"Susan, this is the reason I brought you to this ship ministry— to be a part of this legacy because your life is also impacting many people and generations."* As I listened to the entire story, my heart became filled with awe and wonder because of this revelation I had just received from the Almighty God, our Father, Who has great plans for each one of us.

From 2010 to 2018, I served for a total of five and a half years within two terms. The only year I did not set foot aboard *Logos Hope* was 2015. I first walked up the gangway in March 2010 for my Global Missions Orientation training, and in September 2010, the ship became my home. I walked down the gangway in February 2014, knowing in my heart that God had said, "I am not finished with you yet in this ministry."

Desiring to walk in total obedience and submission to God's will, I walked up the gangway again in May 2016. I am now getting ready to walk down again in April 2018. I stand here today being the first believer in my generation as well as the first missionary in my family lineage. God used my life to break generational curses and to set new generational trends as I point others to Jesus Christ our Savior and Redeemer.

I give Daddy God praise and thanks for all that He has done in and through my life for the last two years. He created opportunities on board for me to serve in different capacities such as the bookfair, help ministry, onboard events, people development, OM Caribbean, and hotel and catering division.

Some highlights

- Seeing some amazing places and sharing hope with people (*twenty-five* countries and *thirty-six* ports)
- Sailing through the Atlantic Ocean en route to the Caribbean region
- Experiencing the beautiful Caribbean islands and cultures
- Divine connections in each port, especially in the Caribbean region
- Sailing into my beautiful country and hearing how people enjoyed the local food
- Recruiting and motivating people into missions and encouraging them to *pray, give*, and *go*.
- Welcoming all the new recruits on board from the Caribbean

- Being able to mentor, coach, and encourage some of the younger ladies on board
- Being able to reconnect with some former Bible school colleagues during the Caribbean tour
- Being a ministry trainer for new crew members PST Tema

Some lowlights
- Limited personal space
- Almost got burned out at the end of Jamaica (God opened the door for me to return home.)
- Having to say goodbye to friends each changeover was emotionally draining

I wish to thank
- Daddy God for sustaining me over the last two years. He has been faithful to me.

He is truly my rock of all ages.

Isaiah 26:4 (KJV), "Trust in the Lord forever: for in the Lord Jehovah is everlasting strength."

He is my anchor that holds.

Hebrews 6:19, "This hope is a strong and trustworthy anchor for our souls, it leads us through the curtain into God's inner sanctuary."

He is my shield and buckler.

Psalm 18:2 (KJV), "The Lord is my rock, and my fortress, and my deliverer; my God, my strength, in whom I will trust; my buckler, and the horn of my salvation, and my high tower."

- All my faithful supporters and prayer partners
- The leaders for giving me the opportunity to serve in different capacities on board. This quote helps me on my journey with God: "If you see something that you don't like, then change it. If you cannot change it, then change the way you think about it." I encourage you to pray for the leaders and ask God to help you to pray, especially when you feel helpless in a situation on board the ship.
- All divisions and departments for their hard work and service to the Lord
- Everyone who made my time on board memorable (cabin mates; Sandra and Grace).
- All the Caribbean people who served with me during my time on board/Papua New Guinea (PNG) family
- Everyone who shared their stories with me and allowed me to speak into their lives
- My wonderful ship family the "De Lima" who adopted me into their family

My next step
- I leave the ship on April 24 and travel to Curaçao for a month-long vacation before returning to Trinidad where I

will reconnect with my family, friends, and supporting churches. I will then be exploring some opportunities that became available to me.

You can pray
- That I will have a smooth reentry back home reconnecting with family and friends
- That I will continue to walk in God's perfect will for my life
- That God will continue to supply all my needs according to His riches in glory by Christ Jesus

God bless you all and continue to seek God and love Him with all your heart, soul, and mind, which can be summed up in Jeremiah 29:13 (NKJV), "And you will seek me and find me, when you search for me with all your heart."

In His service,
Susan Isidore

CHAPTER 6

God through the Generations

Discovering Myself through My Maternal Lineage

Psalm 90: 1–2 says, "Lord, through all the generations you have been our home! Before the mountains were born, before you gave birth to the earth and the world, from beginning to end, you are God."

As a child growing up, I did not think much about my family's history or much of the origin of my name. I just knew that I was called a "Cocoa Panyol," and I was from a quaint little village named Paramin. This village is nestled in the northern range of Trinidad and Tobago and overlooks the village of Maraval as well as some areas of Diego Martin and Port of Spain. The Panyols are defined as "an ethnic group in Trinidad and Tobago of mixed Spanish, Amerindian, Afro-Latin American, and Afro-Trinidadian and Tobagonian descent."

I never met my maternal grandmother's father (my great-grandfather), but I remembered my grandmother saying that her father whom she called Papa Francois was from Martinique. My grandmother the late Mildred Isidore and my grandfather the late John B. Nicholas were never married; therefore, all her children carried the surname ISIDORE. My mother, Victoria Isidore, and my father, Martin Constantine, were also not married, so I carried my mother's last name. This is how I got my surname ISIDORE, which originates from Greek and means "strong gift."

As the years went by and life continued, I still did not think much about my name until one of the guys at Bible school referred to me as a Spanish girl with a French name. This got my attention, and I started thinking more about the origin of my name and my family's history. During that same time, there was another student from Bible school whose surname was also ISIDORE, and he was from Saint Lucia.

On occasions, some people would come up to us and ask if we were related, and we would jokingly say, "We were from a pumpkin vine family—only connected by the same surname." While conversing with this gentleman, he informed me that there are many people from Saint Lucia with the surname ISIDORE. This information further piqued my curiosity about the origin of my name.

In 2016, when I left Trinidad to go back to the mission field, little did I know that Father God had plans to take me on a journey that would lead to the discovery of the origin of my family name. This journey began in the port of Ghana. There was a group of new recruits who came aboard in the Short-Term Exposure Program (STEP). In this group, there was a certain guy who immediately got all excited when he saw the name ISIDORE written on my badge. He said, "My sister, how are you doing?"

I responded to him but was totally surprised by his introduction. He then proceeded to tell me that he was originally from the country of Togo, which is in West Africa, and many people with my surname live in his country. I then shared with him how I received the name ISIDORE, which originated from my great-grandfather who was from Martinique.

Another part of this journey became clear to me when I visited one of the historical sites, the Cape Coast Castle—one of forty "slave castles" or large commercial forts built by European traders on the Gold Coast of Ghana. It was originally built by the Swedes for trade in timber and gold but was later used in the trans-Atlantic slave trade. As we toured the castle, I learned more about the experiences that the slaves endured. At one point, we were placed in a small room with no ventilation. The tour guide wanted the group to experience the discomfort of staying in a closed room with limited space. As she proceeded to close the door, I had to excuse myself from the room. The discomfort of the strong musty smell compounded with a feeling of claustrophobia was a little too much for me to bear at that time.

The journey continued when we left Ghana and sailed to Praia and Mindelo, two ports in the lovely country of Cabo Verde or Cape Verde. This is an island country spanning an archipelago of ten volcanic islands in the central Atlantic Ocean, off the northwest coast of Africa. The population in this country is mostly of mixed European and sub-Saharan African heritage (mulato), which is similar to some of the people of the Caribbean islands. These islands were ideally located for the Atlantic slave trade and grew prosperous during that era. As slavery ended in the nineteenth century, there was a great economic decline and emigration. However, the country gradually recovered as an important commercial center and stopover for shipping routes. After our time in Cape Verde, we sailed to the Canary Islands, spending several days there.

As we left the Canary Islands and sailed for eleven days through the Atlantic Ocean, heading toward the Caribbean islands, I gained more insight into the origin of my name. The voyage was a bit rough at times because the ship's stabilizers stopped working at certain points. On most nights, it was difficult to have a proper rest because of the level of noise emanating from the engine room.

During this voyage, one of my major responsibilities as the OM Caribbean representative was to put together the "area orientation" for the Caribbean region. This orientation is geared toward informing the ship's community about some of the history and other interesting facts about the particular region. Knowledge about the various countries within that region was also included. The orientation also included some *dos* and *don'ts* as it relates to the specific cultures.

As I was preparing my notes and doing further research for the presentation, my ancestral history became much clearer. I was able to see a correlation with all the pieces of information I received from the journey relating to the origin of my family name. The ancestors of my maternal great-grandfather originated from one of the African countries, probably Togo. They were then transported to the Caribbean via the slave trade where they settled in Martinique. After some time, many of these early settlers traveled to Trinidad.

I thanked God for allowing me to learn a little more about my ancestors. He allowed me to learn the history in a personal way and to travel the route that many of them traveled during the slave trade. The slave ships sailed from Ghana to Cabo Verde, where they would have stopped off to receive supplies before continuing their journey through the Atlantic Ocean to the Caribbean. In the year 2016, missionary Susan Jennine

Isidore was privileged to make the same journey that her ancestors made many generations before.

Discovering Myself through My Paternal Lineage

A few years after my conversion, I attended a discipleship session with my spiritual Father the late apostle Bertril Baird. In that session, he highlighted the importance of the relationship between a father and his daughter. As he continued sharing, I began my self-introspection. In my heart, I knew I did not have that kind of relationship with my father. After the session, his words remained with me, and I felt the Lord impress on my heart, saying, "You should seek after this relationship with your father."

I knew my father from a child but did not live with him. I also knew my relatives on his side of the family because they were from the same little village in Paramin. On occasion, I would see my relatives while traveling to and from school or when visiting my maternal grandmother's house. There were also infrequent visits to my paternal grandparents' home—the late Rita and Theodore Constantine.

I was not aware of my father's family history because of the fact that I did not have a close relationship with them. I had a closer bond with my relatives on my mother's side of the family. At one point, my father moved out of Paramin, and I did not see him for several years, nor was I in touch with him. In those early years, cell phones were not as prevalent as they are today, so people did not communicate that often.

In obedience to what Father God said to me, I decided to seek after this relationship with my dad. I made contact with one of my cousins and asked him to take me to visit my dad and my stepmom. I can still remember how surprised they were to see me on that Sunday afternoon when I visited their home in Santa Cruz. This was the beginning of my journey of getting to know more about my father.

After this initial visit, arrangements were made to have monthly visits to my father's home. This was greatly appreciated by my dad, stepmom, and three of my younger siblings. Besides getting to know my dad personally, I also started learning more about myself and the things I would have inherited from him or his side of the family. One trait I inherited is being analytical. I also learned that one of my aunts was an accountant. I was totally surprised by this news because I also worked in the accounting field for several years. During these visits to my dad's home, I was able to develop a greater bond with my siblings. As I got to know them personally, based on their occupations, I saw that most of them inherited my father's analytical trait.

I was thankful to God that He was restoring those things in my life that were absent during my childhood. This was a great feeling and a sense of assurance, knowing that God was working on my behalf. I always loved family life and looked forward to having my own family one day. As the relationship between my father and I was being restored, the relationship between my father and mother was also being restored.

One of my significant moments was being able to have both parents present at my commissioning service in 2010. It felt great having their support in this special venture as I prepared to go to the nations. This was the first time I had both parents present at one of my special occasions. This support continued, as they were both present at the airport for my departure from Trinidad in August 2010. It was also a joy to host them on board the ship when she returned to Trinidad during the Caribbean tour in 2017.

After learning about the history of my mother's side of the family, once again, my curiosity was piqued. I decided to ask my dad where my grandparents originated from. He told me that my grandmother's mother (my great-grandmother) was from Grenada, and her father (my great-grandfather) was from Venezuela. When my dad shared this with me, I had an epiphany because the two countries he mentioned were the countries where I did short-term missions.

I traveled to Venezuela in 2005 and then to Grenada in 2009. As I pondered on this new revelation of my paternal lineage, I immediately realized how privileged I was to set foot on the soil of these two countries, where my great-grandparents walked many generations before. Yet again, I had a grateful heart toward Father God for ordering my steps and for directing my path. "The LORD directs the steps of the godly. He delights in every detail of their life" (Psalm 37:23).

Generational God

In *Mathew 1:2–17*,

> Abraham was the father of Isaac. Isaac was the father of Jacob. Jacob was the father of Judah and his brothers. Judah was the father of Perez and Zerah (whose mother was Tamar). Perez was the father of Hezron. Hezron was the father of Ram. Ram was the father of Amminadab. Amminadab was the father of Nahshon. Nahshon was the father of Salmon. Salmon was the father of Boaz (whose mother was Rahab). Boaz was the father of Obed (whose mother was Ruth).

Obed was the father of Jesse. Jesse was the father of King David. David was the father of Solomon (whose mother was Bathsheba, the widow of Uriah). Solomon was the father of Rehoboam. Rehoboam was the father of Abijah. Abijah was the father of Asa. Asa was the father of Jehoshaphat. Jehoshaphat was the father of Jehoram. Jehoram was the father of Uzziah. Uzziah was the father of Jotham. Jotham was the father of Ahaz. Ahaz was the father of Hezekiah. Hezekiah was the father of Manasseh. Manasseh was the father of Amon. Amon was the father of Josiah. Josiah was the father of Jehoiachin and his brothers (born at the time of the exile to Babylon). After the Babylonian exile: Jehoiachin was the father of Shealtiel. Shealtiel was the father of Zerubbabel. Zerubbabel was the father of Abiud. Abiud was the father of Eliakim. Eliakim was the father of Azor. Azor was the father of Zadok. Zadok was the father of Akim. Akim was the father of Eliud. Eliud was the father of Eleazar. Eleazar was the father of Matthan. Matthan was the father of Jacob. Jacob was the father of Joseph, the husband of Mary. Mary gave birth to Jesus, who is called the Messiah. All those listed above include fourteen generations from Abraham to David, fourteen from David to the Babylonian exile, and fourteen from the Babylonian exile to the Messiah.

As is seen in the above-mentioned scriptures, God saw fit to document all the generations of the lineage from which Jesus came. God is a generational God. When someone comes to the saving knowledge of God through His Son Jesus Christ or "gets saved," He sees this not only as an individual being saved but also as a generation.

"And all of this is a gift from God, who brought us back to himself through Christ. And God has given us this task of reconciling people to him" (2 Corinthians 5:18).

God reconciled me back to Himself and restored my broken relationships. Through the many years of waiting on God and being processed, God was building a foundation for me, upon which my ministry of reconciliation or bringing others to Christ will now be able to stand. God wanted to give me an understanding of my history before allowing me to enter into the future—my promised land. There, I can now build my own family as I move forward with the blessings of Abraham. I am thankful to God for allowing me to trace both my lineages until the fourth generation and for giving me the authority to claim His blessings even from those generations. I look forward to continuing the work of reconciling men to God, especially those from these nations of my ancestors.

The Will of God

"The Lord says, 'I will guide you along the best pathway for your life. I will advise you and watch over you'" (Psalm 32:8).

God has a plan for each of us. Pursuing this plan will not always be easy, because on the journey, we will be faced with opposition and discouragement. The Bible is our guide for God's general plan for man's life and for the specific plan for each of us if we choose to follow Him. When I stepped out in obedience to God, seeking to restore the relationship with my dad, I met with some opposition, but I did not let that deter me. I remained focused and followed through with what God said to me. The road to being obedient to God is sometimes a very lonely one. It is, however, worth it, especially when you know your destiny and legacy would be positively altered by your obedience.

I can also remember when I returned to the ship for my third mission, a number of people asked me, "Why did you return?"

My response was, "Because it is God's will for my life."

One person even asked, "Why didn't you return closer to the time when the ship is supposed to be in the Caribbean?"

Some people knew that the first three and a half years on board was not an easy time for me, but I persevered and pressed through with the help of my Father God. I am a finisher, and I can do all things through Christ Who strengthens me, as the scripture says. When I start something, I like to complete it, and not just complete it—but complete it well. I knew God had a bigger purpose and plan for my life than what people could have seen or understood.

I am glad it was God ordering my steps, not man, so that His purpose was fulfilled in my life during my time on board. I would continually pray God's Word over my life using Paul's word from Philippians 1:6, "And I am certain that God, who began the good work within you, will continue his work until it is finally finished on the day when Christ Jesus returns."

There was opposition and discouragement during my period of brokenness when I chose to give up on the relationship of six and a half years to follow God's plan for my life. However, the scripture that I held onto was from the book of Romans 8:18, "Yet what we suffer now is nothing compared to the glory he will reveal to us later." At that point, I kept telling myself that something good would come out of this emotional pain I was experiencing. Some people who do not believe in God may say all of these experiences in my life are just coincidences, but I can assure you that God is real and that He is interested in the affairs of men, His creation. It is imperative that we trust in the God we cannot see, choose to see what He is revealing, and listen to hear what He is saying to us.

"In his kindness God called you to share in his eternal glory by means of Christ Jesus. So, after you have suffered a little while, he will restore, support, and strengthen you, and he will place you on a firm foundation" (1 Peter 5:10).

At certain points on my journey, there were intense spiritual battles. I had to fight against principalities and powers that wanted to cause divisions and strife with the generation before me. During those times, I also felt I was at a crossroad, having to fight for the generations after me. I was determined not to allow the generations after me to be subject to the same generational curses that affected my life. The enemy did not want me to reach my destiny where I can claim the authority and blessings that God has in store for me, especially the spiritual covering for the next generation.

My journey of waiting on God for breakthroughs has been a long one. There were times of discouragement and weariness mixed with tears. Many times, I cried out to my Heavenly Father, and He always encouraged me through His Word. Encouragement also came from different sources, such as my devotionals, a song, a thought in my spirit from the Holy Spirit, or through someone who would pray for me or with me. There were periods when I did not fully understand what Father God was doing, and I could not see the big picture. In those moments, I had to trust what the Word of God said to me and what was also spoken over my life. The following scriptures are a major part of my spiritual foundation, and they help to encourage me in fulfilling the will of God for my life:

In Psalm 84:11,

> "For the Lord God is our sun and our shield. He gives us grace and glory. The Lord will withhold no good thing from those who do what is right."

In Jeremiah 29:11,

> "For I know the plans I have for you," says the Lord. "They are plans for good and not for disaster, to give you a future and a hope."

In Proverbs 3:5–6,

> "Trust in the Lord with all your heart; do not depend on your own understanding. Seek his will in all you do, and he will show you which path to take."

In Isaiah 40:31,

> "But those who trust in the Lord will find new strength. They will soar high on wings like eagles. They will run and not grow weary. They will walk and not faint."

In Isaiah 41:10,

> "Don't be afraid, for I am with you. Don't be discouraged, for I am your God. I will strengthen you and help you. I will hold you up with my victorious right hand."

In Psalm 46:10,

> "Be still, and know that I am God! I will be honored by every nation. I will be honored throughout the world."

In Psalm 37:23,

> "The LORD directs the steps of the godly. He delights in every detail of their lives."

CHAPTER 7

Waiting for My Husband—My Boaz

Promise of a Husband

"Then the LORD God said, 'It is not good for the man to be alone. I will make a helper who is just right for him'" (Genesis 2:18).

These are some of the questions I faced on my journey:

"Susan, can I ask you a question?"

Sure!

"How is it a beautiful lady like you is not married? Is it that no one ever expressed interest?"

"Susan, how do you do it? You seem to be so comfortable being single. Don't you desire to be married?"

The first question was asked to me by a mature woman from South Africa who was curious about why I was still single.

I responded by saying, "I am still single because I am choosing to wait on the husband God has promised me." My response to the second question was, "Yes, I do desire to be married, but I have learned to trust God as I wait for my husband. The journey of waiting has been a long one, but I do believe it will be all worthwhile because Father God is faithful." I then took the opportunity to share more about my testimony with this young lady from Poland.

My desire to be married and have a family was birthed at thirteen years old while caring for one of my baby cousins. A few months after my conversion, one of the promises that Father God gave me was confirmation that He will provide a husband for me. He also spoke from the Word, indicating that this individual was not living in Trinidad and Tobago but would come from abroad. This prophetic word from God helped to anchor my faith and trust, especially when some of my brothers in Christ expressed their interest in me.

I can remember after a Sunday service when one of the elders from my local church said to me, "Like the men in our church are blind, why are they not seeing a beautiful woman like you?"

I told him, "Do not blame the men because some of them have expressed interest, but God has me waiting for the man that He has chosen for me."

Not being boastful, but truth be told, I would need a second pair of hands to count the number of guys who showed interest in me over the many years while I waited for the chosen one.

Marriage Is for Purpose

There were many lessons I learned on this journey of waiting for my husband. One of them is that marriage has a purpose. When God knits a man and woman together, it is not just to look pretty together or to enjoy beautiful intimacy with each other. I believe the key reason is to fulfill their God-given purpose individually and together as a team. As both individuals help each other to accomplish their life's purpose, their marriage should also reflect a testimony of God's lordship in their lives.

Having been in a committed relationship before, there were things I was not aware of in relation to the principles of the Bible. As a Christian woman, I now had to renew my thinking and learn the correct process related to marriage from a biblical perspective. One of the key things I had to learn was about the "covering" a father has over his daughter. This covering would be transferred from her father to her husband who would now be her cover when she leaves her father's house. Most importantly, her overall covering is from her Heavenly Father. This covering would help her submit to her husband because she has learned to submit to the Word of God. Ultimately, this understanding can lead to a successful relationship and marriage.

"Leave it, maintain it, and trust God to keep it." This phrase was dropped into my spirit in the early part of my journey of waiting for my husband. I felt the Lord saying to me that this is the model He wants me to adopt as it relates to my future spouse. *Leave it*—allow the individual space to continue growing in their personal life with God and with others. In other words, do not contribute to stifling your spouse's personal growth. *Maintain it*—know who you are in Christ. This means it is important to know your spiritual identity. Know what your purpose is for being married. Also, know what your role is as a wife to your husband or vice versa. *Trust God to keep it*—place exclusive trust in God to bring this individual into your life and also to keep him or her in your life.

During my time of waiting, I have been equipping myself to fulfill this position. One of the great and helpful books I read was titled *Lady in Waiting* by authors Jackie Kendall and Debby Jones. In this book, they wrote about the lady in waiting—being a lady of reckless abandonment, a lady of diligence, a lady of faith, a lady of virtue, a lady of devotion, a lady of purity, a lady of security, a lady of contentment, a lady of conviction, and a lady of patience. I can truly say that God has allowed me to be processed in all these areas, and this has helped me to be a well-rounded lady in waiting.

Relationship between Men and Women

Another lesson I learned during my season of waiting was that God's desire for us is to see each other as brothers and sisters in Christ before seeing each other as husband or wife. As we do this, our concern would be more geared toward guarding each other's hearts and desiring to protect each other from sexual sin or traps set by the enemy. God also wants us all to have our primary security in Him before we look for security in other people, including our mate. God wants us always to be totally dependent on Him, seeing Him as our overall source and security. If as an individual, you do not discover who you are and what you were created to do, when you team up with your mate, you would now put extra demands on this individual to fill your voids.

As the Lord started revealing these truths to me, whenever guys approached, my first question to Father God would be, "What is the purpose for bringing this person into my life?" My initial thought was not to see the person as a love interest but first to consider what reason Father God had for making this connection with my brother in Christ. I can attest that there was always a purpose in the connections, so much so that some of these brothers are still my good friends today.

At one point on my journey, I felt emotionally tired when men became interested in me and I could not give them what they desired, which was a wife relationship instead of a sister relationship. As a result, I started taking the approach of praying for wives for my brothers. I felt they were good brothers, and the only challenge was that I was not the wife God had chosen for them. Yes! At times, this was quite difficult. It was also a personal sacrifice because I had to deny myself and my desires while praying for someone else's desires to be fulfilled.

Guarding One's Heart

*Guard your heart above all else, for it
determines the course of your life.*

—Proverbs 4:23

The word *heart* used in this scripture is not referring to the organ in our chest which pumps the blood around our body. Instead, the word *heart* is used to refer to a person's character or the place within a person where feelings or emotions are considered to come from.

A key lesson learned during this season of waiting for my husband is the importance of guarding my heart. The word *guard* can be defined as "to watch over to protect or control." Other words that can be used to define the word *guard* are to shield, to look after, to cover, to keep safe, and to screen.

In the book of Jeremiah, the scripture tells *us*, "The heart is deceitful above all things, and desperately wicked: who can know it?" (Jeremiah 17:9 KJV*)*. It is easy for us to be deceived by our hearts, especially in the area of personal relationships; this is why God has encouraged us to guard our hearts. One of the ways I have been guarding my heart is by screening the types of movies I watch. My favorite movies are romantic comedies, so I have since put those on the shelf until this season of my life is over. The reason for doing this is to protect my heart from desiring intimacy during this season when I am not in a position to pursue it.

Another area of guarding is ensuring that I maintain the right thoughts as they relate to my brothers as well as establishing healthy boundaries during our friendships. It is always good to let guys know what you expect of them and from them. As a woman, you should be clear in expressing what your intentions are for a friendship with a guy to avoid unmet expectations. This is one of the first boundaries that you should set as a woman. If your brother cannot respect your boundaries, then he is not worthy of your presence. When we enter into a relationship with Jesus Christ, we have to do things differently in comparison to how we may have done them when we were in the world and did not have a relationship with Jesus Christ. Practicing these truths has helped me in maintaining my intimacy with the Holy God. The scripture says it this way: "This means that anyone who belongs to Christ has become a new person. The old life is gone; a new life has begun!" (2 Corinthians 5:17).

Continual Prayer for the Promise of my Husband

During these years of waiting, I have been continually praying to receive the promise of a husband. There are times when I become tired of praying and feel like the promise is taking forever to be manifested. However, Father God would always encourage my heart, and I would begin praying again. There were some crazy experiences on this journey of waiting for my promise, and there are still some unanswered questions related to some of these experiences. Nevertheless, what God has been continually saying to me is that I must *wait and trust Him to bring the "promise" into my life.*

Truly, this process of waiting has really been stretching my faith and also teaching me to trust God even when I do not fully understand what He is doing in my life. There were times when I asked Father God, "Why is my process of meeting a spouse so unconventional?" The only answer I received thus far is to trust Him with the process and plans He has for my life.

In June 2019, my heart was encouraged by a word of knowledge from Father God. One of the prophetess in our local church came up to me and said, "*Your prince is coming from abroad*, West Indian. Do not fight it."

My response was, "Thank you very much. I do believe, and I am also in a place of expectancy." I continue to trust a God Who never lies, as it is said in the book of Numbers, "God is not a man, so he does not lie. He is not human, so he does not change his mind. Has he ever spoken and failed to act? Has he ever promised and not carried it through?" (Numbers 23:19).

Today is September 23, 2019, the day on which I celebrated my birthday. As I conclude this chapter, I am expecting the man of promise to walk into my life any time soon. So stay tuned and be excited about my second book. There, you will get to read about my journey of receiving the promise and what the process was like for my husband as he was being prepared to find me—his wife. "The man who finds a wife finds a treasure, and he receives favor from the LORD" (Proverbs 18:22).

CHAPTER 8

Waiting through Transitions

In-Between Season—Level 1

*For everything there is a season, a time
for every activity under heaven.*

—Ecclesiastes 3:1

A transition can be considered the process or a period of changing from one state or condition to another, but I would like to refer to it as an in-between period or season. During this in-between period, you must be totally convinced of what God spoke to you about during your active or mountaintop season. This Word from God is what you will have to hold onto during challenging times.

Throughout this in-between season, though one may be involved in certain activities, it is really a place of learning and preparation for the next level. However, to some people, this period may seem to be inactive, but that's alright; once you know, you are where God wants you to be and are doing what He wants you to do.

Knowing the purpose for which God has created you and is preparing you is very important. It is also imperative that you fully accept the call of God on your life while waiting for the manifestation of a promise or direction for the next step. If you do not fully accept God's call, you can become easily distracted in the direction others may be attempting to lead you in. Acceptance and solidification of your calling will keep you focused on your purpose. This will also give you peace and assurance that God will work on your behalf, and in His timing, all things will be made beautiful. "Yet God has made everything beautiful for its own time. He has planted eternity in the human heart, but even so, people cannot see the whole scope of God's work from beginning to end" (Ecclesiastes 3:11).

I can remember vividly my first in-between season. It was the time when I returned from my first mission trip in 2005. Two days before leaving for the mission trip, I resigned from my job of ten years. When I returned from the trip, I was prepared to receive directions for my next step from the Lord. Here I was, ready to distribute my résumé in search of a new job when I sensed the Lord saying to me, "Do not send out any résumés."

My response was, "How will I get a job if I do not send out any résumés?"

His response was, "Trust Me!"

This act of surrendering was difficult, but I said, "Okay, I will trust You."

The weeks were going by, and nothing seemed to be happening, but I continued trusting as Father God had asked me to. In the sixth week of my in-between season, I was in my room having devotions when I was called to the phone. I answered the call and said, "Hello, good morning!"

The response on the other end of the phone was, "Are you still interested in working with us?"

I was totally surprised by the response because I could not remember sending out any résumé in search of a job. I took the necessary information and told the person I would return their call to confirm my decision. At that point, I did not have any recollection of when I sent out a résumé to that law school. Nevertheless, I returned to my room and continued with my devotions, asking Father God if this was the door He opened for me. I sensed He said yes, so I contacted the institution and had the interview the same afternoon and started working the following day.

My faith and trust in God significantly increased through this experience because I saw Him work on my behalf without my help. About three years prior, I sent out my résumé to that law school after seeing an ad in the newspapers. However, as time passed, I forgot about it and did not expect to get a response three years later.

This job lasted six months but was very intense both physically and spiritually. I remember on the second day asking Father God, "Why did You send me to work in this crazy place?"

His response was, "I need to teach you some lessons, and this is where I want you to learn them."

The lessons that God wanted me to learn were teaching my hands to war spiritually and learning to pray continually, not only for myself but also for the people and the institution. God wanted to take me to another level of intercessory prayer and for me to practice what it means to continually walk in the spirit so that I would not respond in the flesh. Galatians 5:16 says, "So I say, let the Holy Spirit guide your lives. Then you won't be doing what your sinful nature craves." And Psalm

18:34 says, "He trains my hands for battle; he strengthens my arm to draw a bronze bow."

As I shared some of the experiences and challenges I faced on the job, a few people asked me, "Why don't you just leave the job?" I knew that leaving was not an option because Father God had already spoken to me about His purpose for placing me in that position. I had to persevere and learn the lessons that He wanted to teach me. I always believe that the faster we learn the lessons God is teaching us, the sooner our breakthroughs and promotions would happen.

Working at the institution was not all bad. God also used me as a source of encouragement to the boss during the death of one of her best friends. I was also called upon to pray during one of the special events at the school, and most of all, I was able to be a positive influence on the young students and staff.

After many experiences and lessons learned, the time came when I got the release from Father God to leave the institution. I was totally surprised and moved by the gifts I received from my colleagues and students at the school. I would often say that the six months of working at the institution felt like six years, but the testimony that I left behind was glorifying God.

There would be times when God wants us to be in a place we may not like, but we must remember that He is always about the bigger picture when it comes to us fulfilling our purpose. God will do whatever is necessary, sending us to places and putting us into positions that He deems fit to process and equip us for our destiny and purpose.

In-Between Season—Level 2

One of the things we will notice on our journey with God is that there is never a dull moment or a period of stagnation.

God is always keeping us engaged while preparing us for the next level. Our journey will consist of many levels with God, and the preceding levels will help equip us for the next level. The levels in life will continually increase until we reach the end of our earthly journey.

After my time off work, I had a nice vacation week in Tobago. I then returned to Trinidad, asking Father God, "What's next?" This in-between season was a bit more challenging and lasted eight months. This lesson of trusting God went to another level. I kept my focus because I believed Father God had worked everything out in the previous season of my life, and He was able to do it once again.

During these eight months, God taught me to see Him as my Jehovah-Jireh—the God who provides. Since I started working at the age of twenty-one, I knew what it was to receive a salary from the bank at the end of every month. However, during this season, I had to adapt to this aspect of my life and totally depend on my Father God to pay all my bills.

During that time, I lived in the dormitory at the Bible school I attended prior. I enjoyed having my room, and it was a pleasure sharing the other facilities with some lovely ladies. To date, a couple of them are still a part of my life and journey. Each month, God provided in different ways through different people, and I was totally grateful for all His provisions. This was a lean season in my life, and God taught me to live out the scripture that says, "But Jesus told him [the devil], No! The scripture says 'people do not live by bread alone, but by every word that comes from the mouth of God'" (Matthew 4:4).

All my life, I always had more than enough to eat; however, throughout these months, there were occasions when I had to eat very sparingly even though I desired more at times. During this season, I can truly say I learned what it was to be hungry. I encouraged myself using these words: "This too shall pass because it's only for a season."

Having gone through this season of my life, I can now empathize with those who suffer from hunger or who may be going through a season of leanness. One of the greatest lessons Father God taught me during this season was that He is my main source. He will use different people to bless His children, but He will never allow anyone to take His glory for assisting with the provision of those needs. My love and appreciation for God grew even more as a result of this lesson. The Lord promised to supply all our needs according to Paul in Philippians 4:19, "And this same God who takes care of me will supply all your needs from his glorious riches, which have been given to us in Christ Jesus."

At certain points throughout this season, a few people asked, "Don't' you want a job?"

I responded, "Yes, I do want to work, but God is telling me to wait on Him."

After hearing this question a few times, I felt a bit discouraged, but I knew God told me to wait on Him, and I was doing just that. This time of waiting was not easy. One day, as I was reading through the book of Genesis, my faith was encouraged as I read about Abraham's journey when he had to leave his servants behind on the way to sacrifice his son Isaac. From this, I learned that Abraham had to continue the journey by himself because his faith was being tested. This greatly encouraged my heart, and my faith in God became more tangible. I realized that this was my test of faith and trust. It was okay if other people did not believe in me because this test was not for others but only for God and me.

As the months went by, I continued waiting on God. I also got involved in a few activities that I felt the Lord was directing. One of these areas I believe was for me to enroll in classes to further my studies in accounting. One day, around the seventh month of waiting, I had a dream where I received keys from one of the lecturers at the Bible school. Immediately, I had this feeling that my next job would be working at the Bible school.

Within two weeks, I received a telephone call from the school inviting me to apply for a vacant position as a receptionist. I knew this door was from Father God, so I sent in my résumé, had the interview, and got accepted for the position. During this time, around the month of October 2006, my pastor, the late Apostle Joshua Turnel Nelson, went home to glory to be with the Lord. This was a sad time for our fellowship, but we knew that God was in control and that He is Sovereign, so we trusted His purpose and plans for the fellowship.

I started work at the Bible school as the receptionist at the beginning of November 2006. After working in that position for six months, the door was opened for me to fill the position of director of business. I worked closely with the president and was responsible for managing the finances for the Bible school. In that new role, I also had to provide financial reports for the board meetings of the school.

My pastor, the late Apostle Joshua Turnel Nelson, used to be part of this same board during his tenure as the general bishop for the Pentecostal Assemblies of the West Indies (PAWI) fellowship. I saw this as a significant position God had prepared for me to serve His people. This felt like a position where I was representing my late pastor, and as a result, I felt humbled by what God was doing in my life.

I can also remember when some people learned about my position at the Bible school and said to me, "You are very lucky because you are working three minutes away from where you live."

I told them, "This is not about being lucky, but it's about having your steps ordered by Father God and waiting on His timing." "The LORD directs the steps of the godly. He delights in every detail of their lives" (Psalm 37:23).

In-Between Season—Reentry

Reentry is the act of entering again into your own home and culture after spending a long time on the mission field. This could be likened to a space shuttle returning from space and penetrating through the earth's atmosphere. If you do not have a proper support system with understanding, love, and encouragement, your reentry process can be very difficult. This transition can be a very stressful time, and if not handled well, it can also become a very depressing time. One of the keys to having a smooth reentry is being honest with yourself and the people around you. It is important that everyone is informed of your true feelings, ensuring that church leaders, family, and friends do not have unrealistic expectations of you.

In February 2014, during the wee hours of the morning, I left my floating home, the *Logos Hope* ship, in the port of Bangkok, Thailand. There I was, sitting in the taxi heading to the airport, feeling broken and empty. I had given all that I had on the mission field and was now heading back home into the unknown. The unknown can be a very daunting place because you do not know what to expect and what will be expected of you. This is a season or time when all you can do is trust the one who sees the unknown, the one who is alpha and omega—the beginning and the end.

After traveling for one day, I touched down at the Piarco airport and was greeted by my brother Ovil, along with my dear friends Jennifer and Gilbert. For the initial stages of my reentry, I spent three and a half months at Jennifer's home where I had some time of solitude as I settled back into life in Trinidad. My prayer life and my worship were on the empty gauge during that time. I found myself telling Father God that I did not understand what He was doing in my life. He then reminded me of these two scriptures, which He had given to me during my time on board:

> "For the mountains shall depart, And the hills be removed, But My kindness shall not depart from you, Nor shall My covenant of peace be removed, says the LORD, who has mercy on you" (Isaiah 54:10 NKJV).

> "And the peace of God, which surpasses all understanding, will guard your hearts and minds through Christ Jesus" (Philippians 4:7 NKJV).

God was reminding me that the peace that He has clothed me with surpasses my understanding, so even if I did not understand, it was okay. I just had to trust Him and rest in His peace. I kept telling Father God that I wanted to get back to the place of worship where my heart could once again feel the open flow of our relationship. Instead, there was a block in my worship with God because of the emptiness I was experiencing at the time.

During the first week in Trinidad, I did not go outdoors. I stayed at home and slept. During this time, I received short periods of emotional strength when I made calls informing people of my return. I am glad Father God really knows what we need and when we need it. By the second week, Jennifer invited me to their Friday night service, and I accompanied her.

At the end of the service, the pastor invited people to the altar to receive prayer. I decided to answer the call for prayer. After the pastor prayed, I felt the release and breakthrough to worship Father God once again. As the days went by, I pressed through my initial feelings of emptiness. I started reflecting on what the Lord had done in and through my life over the past three and a half years.

I visited the church once again, for their Sunday morning service. During that time, my worship to God was further strengthened, thereby rekindling my heart of worship. I enjoyed my short stay at Jennifer's home, and God used that time for us to be a blessing and an encouragement to each other. During that time, Father God also worked it out when another friend of mine on vacation; made himself available to take me to the beach and other places of interest on our beautiful island. After my initial three and a half months of rest, I was back at the same place, asking Father God, "What's next?"

Once again, He directed me back to the dormitory at the Bible school and said to me, "Wait on him and be a watchman for the school while you wait."

"Now son of man, I am making you a watchman for the people of Israel. Therefore, listen to what I say and warn them for me" (Ezekiel 33:7).

In-Between Season—Preparation Time

One of the other aspects we need to know about the in-between season is that it is a time of preparation. As God continues to prepare us for the next level, He is also preparing the next level to accommodate us. It is a time of preparation on both sides of the fence. One of the phrases that I would use at times during my journey of waiting is "the wait is weighty." What I mean by this is that there are times when the period of waiting feels overwhelming and can be frustrating, especially when you do not understand all that is happening in the unseen.

During these times, we must learn to encourage ourselves in the Lord just as David did. This can be found in the scriptures.

> "And David was greatly distressed, for the people spoke of stoning him, because the soul of all the people was grieved, every man for his sons and for his daughters: but David encouraged himself in the LORD his God" (1 Samuel 30:6 KJV).

The preparation process will be determined by the size of the vision God has given you. If the call and purpose of your life are great, the waiting process will be longer. This will entail more preparation as God is developing a great foundation for Him to build upon.

In the world of flora, the taller the tree, the deeper the roots must be placed under the earth to withstand all the storms it will face in its lifetime. According to research, Chinese bamboo takes four years to grow underground before you see the tree in the fifth year. When the tree is seen above ground, it grows about eighty feet tall in just six weeks. In the world of fauna, the gestation period for the larger animals will take longer because of the size of the newborn animal that has to be birthed. The African elephant carries the young ones for twenty-two months before giving birth, and they only give birth to one at a time. In the world of construction, the higher the building, the deeper the foundation must go to support the weight of the structure that will be built on it. The tallest building in the world is the Burj Khalifa with a height of 2,717 feet, and its foundation is 164 feet deep, weighing more than 110,000 tons of concrete and steel.

We can see from all these examples in nature and the physical world that there is an order in how things are accomplished.

Likewise, in the spiritual realm, God has an order in how He prepares us. I had the privilege to visit the Burj Khalifa building in 2011 during the ship's visit to Dubai. It is really a beautiful sight, especially when the dancing fountain is being displayed.

I spent a little over two years in the dormitory before leaving again for the mission field in 2016. During this in-between season, I had eight months of rest before God opened a door of employment where I worked for five months. I also pursued an online English program titled Teaching English to Speakers of Other Languages (TESOL). This knowledge further equipped me for the mission field.

Finally, I was able to work for another three months just before leaving for the field. This income was very helpful in covering my living expenses and other expenses in preparation for the field. There were also opportunities for ministry in several churches. All in all, Father God continued to strengthen me for my journey. Yet again, during this time of waiting for over two years, my faith was stretched like Abraham's. However, I held on to my faith and trust as I believed Father God to bring the manifestation of what He had spoken over my life. In the end, I can testify that He did not disappoint.

"God is not a man, so he does not lie. He is not human, so he does not change his mind. Has he ever spoke and failed to act? Has he ever promised and not carried it through?" (Numbers 23:19).

CHAPTER 9

Lessons Learned through Seasons of Waiting

Overcame Insecurities

I have always been a very focused young lady with a melancholy, phlegmatic personality type. Like most people, I also had some insecurities I needed to overcome. The first insecurity I had to deal with was a feeling of discomfort when I was placed in the forefront.

I am the type of person who preferred to work behind the scene. I have the gift of communicating, and I also enjoy talking to people; however, I prefer doing one-on-one rather than being in the front, noticeable to everyone. I remember when I was enrolled in Bible school, I would comment of being happy to not be on the podium to minister; however, this was not God's desire for me. Whenever my colleagues and I went out on a school assignment, I was chosen many times to be up front. I remember saying to one lecturer that I do not like being up front. His response to me was, "The more you try to avoid being in front, the more God will push you forward if this is His will for your life." I took note of his words, and I can truly say that God honored them because this is exactly what happened throughout my time at Bible school.

I could remember quite clearly, during one semester, sitting in my room, thinking about God calling me to be up front preaching His Word. I continued to struggle with this thought and had not fully accepted this fact. During this time, I started reading one of my textbooks for the course called leadership principles. In this book, the author wrote of his desire to be in the background and not up front, but then God told him that he was created to be a leader. The author then shared that he decided to accept God's will for his life. These words spoke directly to my heart almost as if I was writing them. I then told God my heart and asked Him to help me accept His will for my life, especially in having to be up front preaching His Word.

God then confirmed His Word for me about my calling to preach from the book of Isaiah, "And he hath made my mouth like a sharp sword; in the shadow of his hand hath he hid me, and made me a polished shaft; in his quiver hath he hid me" (Isaiah 49:2 KJV). I can honestly say that I have accepted the call on my life to preach the Word of God, and I have become more confident and comfortable doing this over the years. At times, I still prefer being in the background; nevertheless, when Father God opens the door for me to minister, I walk in and allow the Holy Spirit to help me fulfill my God-given purpose.

During my years of waiting, one of the other lessons God solidified in my heart was the importance of focusing on my inner beauty more than my outward beauty. I have always been petite in stature, which was inherited from my mother. Among my grandparents' eleven children, two of them are petite, and my mother happens to be one of them. I had to learn to become comfortable with the body type that Father God gave me, even though I wish there were things I could have changed.

Over the years, I have learned to love myself for who I am, with all my imperfections and frailties, because I understand that Father God loves me just the way He created me. God is more interested in our inner beauty as it relates to our hearts being pure before Him than our outward beauty, which would fade over time. Our inner beauty, which comes from the renewed spirit we receive after accepting Christ, will continue to radiate on the outside as we age gracefully throughout our lifespan. Part of this inner beauty is formed when we are honest with God, with ourselves, and with one another. This is what he desires from all His children. Our intimacy with this Holy God will be maintained when we have a heart filled with honesty, humility, and faith. God led me to the book of Psalm to further reinforce what He said to me about my inner beauty.

In Psalm 45:13 (KJV),

> The king's daughter is all glorious within:
> her clothing is of wrought gold.

In Psalm 51:6 (NKJV),

> Behold, you desire truth in the inward
> parts: and in the hidden part you shall make
> me to know wisdom.

In Psalm 15:1–2 (NKJV),

> Lord, who may abide in your tabernacle?
> Who may dwell in your holy hill? He who

walks uprightly, and works righteousness,
and speaks the truth in his heart.

Solidified My Identity in Christ

I am a child of the Most High God, created in His image and likeness. He has paid a great price to redeem me from the kingdom of darkness to be with Him in the kingdom of light. Even if no one else loves me, I know that my Heavenly Father loves me with an unconditional, everlasting love. This is a short summary of what I believe and what I have built my foundation upon as it relates to who I am and what God has done for me.

Having grown up in a mixed culture and community in Paramin village, I knew my ethnicity was varied. Some of my mothers' sisters further added to this variation when they got married to men of East Indian descent, and because of this fact, my cousins' ethnicity was even more varied. This cultural orientation caused me to grow up seeing people for who they are and not based on the color of their skin and eyes or the texture of their hair. I saw everyone as a unique human being. I then lived in the dormitory at the Bible school that housed students from other Caribbean islands, so there again, it was easy to interact with people of different cultures and backgrounds. This further enhanced me as a person to appreciate who I am and where I came from and also to appreciate the same in others.

I was never one to fail exams, but while pursuing further accounting studies, I failed two of my exams. This was very disappointing because I had to repeat these courses, and the fees were exorbitant. Amid this discouragement, God used this experience to teach me that *qualifications or certificates do not define me; it's only what He says about me that defines me.*

This was a significant lesson for me because, once again, I saw how God uses everything in our lives to work for our good and for His teaching purposes. This experience really helped solidify my identity. I understood my identity was based on God defining me, not what people say about me or what the world system may say to me. This revelation brought a further sense of freedom from wanting to be validated by others, as well as a sense of assurance to keep trusting God to direct my path. The second time around, I passed my exams. In the end, I completed my courses and learned a great life lesson from Father God.

When the time came to go on the mission field, I was settled in for who I am. This helped me adapt to life aboard *Logos Hope* much more easily. I lived with people from over sixty nationalities. It did not matter what assignment I was asked to perform; to me, it was a task that did not necessarily define who I am. Some people did not always appreciate me for who I represented, which sometimes did hurt my feelings. Nevertheless, I did not allow this lack of appreciation to deter me from being confident in who I am. In the end, the only thing that really mattered was what Father God said to me.

Because of my appearance, there were people in places such as South Africa, Cape Verde, the Canary Islands, and the Dominican Republic who believed I could fit into their culture. On the ship, there were four other persons from my country. At times, people would comment that my accent was not as strong as that of the other Trinidadians. Some other people would also comment that I am not like the typical Caribbeans because I am more disciplined about being on time.

While I appreciated the fact that I looked like a local in some of the countries, I am thankful to God that He settled my identity in Him, so I was not moved by any of these voices trying to define me as a person. I usually do not like being labeled, and most times, I am hesitant to follow the crowd. My goal in life is to continually strive to serve with the spirit of excellence because we serve an excellent God. Whatever we are called to do should be done with an excellent spirit as unto God and not unto men. "Work willingly at whatever you do, as though you were working for the Lord rather than for people" (Colossians 3:23).

I do not go after titles or positions; instead, I focus on being where God wants me to be and producing fruit that would remain. Jesus did not speak about titles and positions, but He did speak about every tree being known by its own fruit.

In Luke 6:44–45,

> A tree is identified by its fruit; figs are never gathered from thornbushes, and grapes are not picked from bramble bushes. A good person produces good things from the treasury of a good heart, and an evil person produces evil things from the treasury of an evil heart. What you say flows from what is in your heart.

The Importance of Praying

"Pray in the Spirit at all times and on every occasion. Stay alert and be persistent in your prayers for all believers everywhere" (Ephesians 6:18).

In simple terms, praying is communicating with your Heavenly Father and allowing Him to communicate with you through His Holy Spirit. There is no specific place or posture for praying. The key is to be conscious with an open mind to hear from God. You can talk to Him any time of the day or night. However, there should be occasions that we set aside for prayer time in our secret rooms, allowing us to meet with God. During these sessions, we should focus mainly on fellowship while we seek direction for our life and also make prayers and petitions on behalf of others.

Over the years, I have enjoyed communicating with my Heavenly Father. I always look forward to talking with Him and hearing His voice. At night, I would spend time in devotions reading my Bible, along with other devotionals, as I anticipated what Father God would say to me through His written Word. During the wee hours of the morning, I would have intentional prayer time with my Father. I would spend time in worship and fellowship, after which I would pray for specific requests for myself and others. During this time, Father God would also infuse into my spirit some of the things He wanted me to pray for.

How do I know what the Lord wants me to pray for? At the beginning of my prayer time, I am never certain about what to pray for. However, as I continue to worship, the Holy Spirit would download in my spirit specific things that He wants me to pray for. The more time we spend meditating and studying the Word of God, the easier it will be to discern God's voice as He speaks to us daily. The key to successful prayer is being able to use God's Word to remind Him of what He has said. The Word of God is what would also defeat the devil when he brings thoughts into our minds. We need to believe the Word as we speak it to the enemy, just as Jesus did during His times of testing and trials.

In *Mathew 4:1–11,*(NIV)

> Then Jesus was led by the Spirit into the
> wilderness to be tempted by the devil. After
> fasting forty days and forty nights, he was

hungry. The tempter came to him and said, "If you are the Son of God, tell these stones to become bread." Jesus answered, "It is written: 'Man shall not live on bread alone, but on every word that comes from the mouth of God.'" Then the devil took him to the holy city and had him stand on the highest point of the temple. "If you are the Son of God," he said, "throw yourself down. For it is written: 'He will command his angels concerning you, and they will lift you up in their hands, so that you will not strike your foot against a stone.'" Jesus answered him, "It is also written: 'Do not put the Lord your God to the test.'" Again, the devil took him to a very high mountain and showed him all the kingdoms of the world and their splendor. "All this I will give you," he said, "if you will bow down and worship me." Jesus said to him, "Away from me, Satan! For it is written: 'Worship the Lord your God, and serve him only.'" Then the devil left him, and angels came and attended him.

It has also been a great joy to be able to pray on behalf of others and see God work in their favor. Many of the prayer requests for direction, healing, or provision of a particular need were answered in a timely fashion. One other key area that has helped me on this journey is having covenanted prayer partners. Covenanted prayer partners are people who God has divinely connected to me so that we would stand in the gap for one another. This has really been helpful to me, especially during the low periods of my journey. It's always good to know that you are being prayed for, and the other person also knows that you are covering them in prayer.

I could remember talking to God one night about a major decision I had to make. When I woke up the following morning, these two lines from the song by Bob Marley came into my spirit, "Don't worry about a thing, 'cause every little thing is gonna be alright." I did not have this song in my mind, nor did I hear it in the past few days, so I took note of the words. Shortly thereafter, I left my room and went to the living room area, and there on the television was a program with the theme song "Don't Worry 'Bout a Thing" by Bob Marley. I immediately felt that God was speaking to me through the words in this song. God was telling me not to worry about a thing because it's all going to work out. This settled my heart, and I had the assurance that God was directing my steps in the right direction as it pertained to the decision I had to make.

I know some people might be asking how God can speak to us through a song that is not considered to be a Christian song. My viewpoint on this subject is that God is a God of truth, and all truth comes from Him. He can decide to speak to us through any medium He desires because He is sovereign. A message of truth concerning an answer to prayer can be received from a song, a movie, a billboard, an advertisement, or any other avenue from which the truth is being conveyed. The key is to be open to hearing the truth that is being communicated, and if it's what God is speaking to you, it will bear witness with your spirit. This message will also be confirmed in the mouth of two or three witnesses, or it will be communicated a second or third time. In this way, you will know that God is speaking, and He wants you to receive the truth of the words spoken.

In the book of John, Jesus's words to His disciples about Him being the truth reads,

"Don't let your hearts be troubled. Trust in God, and trust also in me. There is more than enough room in my Father's home. If this were not so, would I have told you that I am going to prepare a place for you? When everything is ready, I will come and get you, so that you will always be with me where I am. And you know the way to where I am going. "No, we don't know, Lord," Thomas said. "We have no idea where you are going, so how can we know the way?" Jesus told him, "I am the way, the truth, and the life. No one can come to the Father except through me. If you had really known me, you would know who my Father is. From now on, you do know him and have seen him!" Philip said, "Lord, show us the Father, and we will be satisfied." Jesus replied, "Have I been with you all this time, Philip, and yet you still don't know who I am? Anyone who has seen me has seen the Father! So why are you asking me to show him to you? Don't you believe that I am in the Father and the Father is in me? The words I speak are not my own, but my Father who lives in me does his work through me. Just believe that I am in the Father and the Father is in me. Or at least believe because of the work you have seen me do" (John 14:1–11).

"Let love be your highest goal! But you should also desire the special abilities the Spirit gives—especially the ability to prophesy. For if you have the ability to speak in tongues, you will be talking only to God, since people won't be able to understand you. You will be speaking by the power of the Spirit; but it will all be mysterious" (1 Corinthians 14:1–2).

One of the other aspects of prayer that I have greatly benefited from is being able to communicate with my Heavenly Father in my heavenly language—speaking in unknown tongues. One year after my conversion, I received this precious spiritual gift, and I am thankful to the Holy Spirit for blessing me with it. During the wee hours of the morning, I would usually start my time of fellowship with Father God, just speaking in my heavenly language. After some time, I would use my normal English language to continue my time in prayer.

Speaking in my heavenly language also helps me to stay focused and not be easily distracted by other noises or thoughts that may try to invade my mind during my time of prayer. There are other times when I would be feeling low or discouraged, and after spending some quality time speaking in my heavenly language, my spirit would be lifted as I would become strengthened and encouraged.

The Importance of Fasting

And there by the Ahava Canal, I gave orders for all of us to fast and humble ourselves before our God. We prayed that he would give us a safe journey and protect us, our children, and our goods as we traveled. For I was ashamed to ask the king for soldiers and horsemen to accompany us and protect us from enemies along the way. After all, we had told the king, "Our God's hand of protection is on all who worship him, but his fierce anger rages against those who abandon him." So we fasted and earnestly prayed that our God would take care of us, and he heard our prayer.

—Ezra 8:21–23

Fasting is another key area that has helped me in maintaining my intimacy with Father God over the years. Fasting is a discipline that helps to deny the flesh and bring it into subjection to the Holy Spirit, thereby strengthening our spirit at the same time. Fasting usually works best when combined with prayer. As you deny the flesh, you then need to feed the spirit by meditating on the Word of God and communicating with God through intentional prayer. Among other things, fasting is beneficial for the consecration of your relationship with God, receiving promises from God, and also for igniting the manifested power of God in one's life. Fasting is not only useful for spiritual growth but also has many health benefits.

You can fast from a variety of things, including food, sweet drinks, social media, movies, or any other area of fleshly desires that may be controlling or overpowering your life. Anything in our lives that we give more attention to than God is considered to be an idol. Fasting to gain discipline in these areas would be a good place to begin. By denying the flesh, you are humbling yourself before God and showing Him that you desire to love Him more than the things of this world or the things that have control over your life.

About two years after my conversion, there was a visiting minister at our local church who spoke about the importance and benefits of fasting. After hearing this message, I have intentionally inculcated the discipline of fasting into my life. Since that time, I would fast for one day each week from after dinner until 6:00 p.m. the following day. This discipline has really helped in maintaining my spiritual connectivity with Father God.

There were times when God desired that my fast be increased to more than one day because this was needed to overcome some intense battles and to get an immediate break-through. On another occasion, He led me into sugar fast because I needed to get some discipline in managing my sugar intake. During this time, I gave up a lot of the sweet things I enjoyed such as chocolates with nuts and cakes. After this period of fasting, my desire for sweet snacks were no longer there. I gained victory over those sugar snacks I enjoyed very much. I now indulge myself occasionally as compared to weekly.

CHAPTER 10

The Importance of Sowing While Waiting

Don't be misled—you cannot mock the justice of God. You will always harvest what you plant. Those who live only to satisfy their own sinful nature will harvest decay and death from that sinful nature. But those who live to please the Spirit will harvest everlasting life from the Spirit. So let's not get tired of doing what is good. At just the right time we will reap a harvest of blessing if we don't give up.

—Galatians 6:7–9

The principle in the Word of God is true for every area of our lives. Whatever we sow—whether in thoughts, words, or deeds— will bring forth fruit after its own kind. We are, therefore, encouraged to sow good seeds, especially during the season of waiting. We also need to remember that the seeds sown may not immediately bring forth fruits, but we can rest assured that once we have sown, the fruit will come forth in God's perfect timing. Another important factor is that most times when we sow into a person's life or ministry, be it financial or otherwise, God at times uses someone else to sow into our lives. The return blessings may not necessarily come from the same person.

During my journey of waiting on God, I have sown into my life by investing in the things of God, such as attending seminars and training programs and purchasing books, CDs, and many other resources. These things have greatly helped me grow in my faith and knowledge of God. Reading has always been my hobby; therefore, I enjoyed investing in my life through the purchase of books. This hobby was further fueled when I lived on board the *Logos Hope*, which is called the world's largest floating bookfair. Interestingly, it was given this tagline because it is the only floating bookfair in the world.

I see the acquiring of knowledge through reading as an asset, which also increases wisdom and further enhances one's life. God, through His Holy Spirit, used many books to be my mentor while I was aboard the ship. He would direct me to the right book at the right time in the right season. After gaining wisdom, insights, and foresight from the books, I would then pass on this knowledge through conversations. I would also recommend these said books to some of the younger women whom I had the opportunity to mentor. I love empowering people and always enjoyed the opportunity to share with others what I have learned or currently learning.

Over the years, I have also maintained the principle of sowing financial seeds into the lives of other missionaries. While practicing this, at the back of my mind, I would often think that one day, I would also need someone to sow into my life. I can honestly say that for all the years that I have been a career missionary, God has been faithful in providing for my financial needs.

Each month, my sponsors maintained their commitment to my support. I consider these financial supporters to be partners, because without their continual support, I could not have been on the field fulfilling my God-given purpose. I always had enough support that I could be a blessing to others. During my time on the field, I also continued giving faithfully toward certain needs that came to my attention.

Another key area where I have maintained the principle of sowing is in the area of tithing—10 percent of earnings or gifts received. This tithe could be given to a local assembly or given toward a particular need or project as directed by the Holy Spirit. The following scriptures speak to the principle of tithing:

In *Leviticus 27:30–32*,

> One-tenth of the produce of the land, whether grain from the fields or fruit from the trees, belongs to the LORD and must be set apart to him as holy. If you want to buy back the LORD's tenth of the grain or fruit, you must pay its value, plus 20 percent. Count off every tenth animal from your herds and flocks and set them apart for the LORD as holy.

In *Hebrews 7:1–10*,

> This Melchizedek was king of the city of Salem and also a priest of God Most High. When Abraham was returning home after winning a great battle against the kings,

Melchizedek met him and blessed him. Then Abraham took a tenth of all he had captured in battle and gave it to Melchizedek. The name Melchizedek means "king of justice," and king of Salem means "king of peace." There is no record of his father or mother or any of his ancestors—no beginning or end to his life. He remains a priest forever, resembling the Son of God. Consider then how great this Melchizedek was. Even Abraham, the great patriarch of Israel, recognized this by giving him a tenth of what he had taken in battle. Now the law of Moses required that the priests, who are descendants of Levi, must collect a tithe from the rest of the people of Israel,[1] who are also descendants of Abraham. But Melchizedek, who was not a descendant of Levi, collected a tenth from Abraham. And Melchizedek placed a blessing upon Abraham, the one who had already received the promises of God. And without question, the person who has the power to give a blessing is greater than the one who is blessed. The priests who collect tithes are men who die, so Melchizedek is greater than they are, because we are told that he lives on. In addition, we might even say that these Levites—the ones who collect the tithe—paid a tithe to Melchizedek when their ancestor Abraham paid a tithe to him. For although Levi wasn't born yet, the seed from which he came was in Abraham's body when Melchizedek collected the tithe from him.

As I have honored God's principles over the years in giving back to Him and His work, I have seen His continued faithfulness in my life. God's blessings would always surpass my expectations, which resulted in me having some crazy faith testimonies, showcasing God's provision and faithfulness.

I would now share one of these testimonies with you. I have a good friend who became my sister in the Lord after leading her to Christ many years ago. We worked together at the same company. In 2014, she prayed and asked God to send her a spiritual mentor, and this was just around the same time I returned to Trinidad from the *Logos Hope* ship. I gladly agreed to become her mentor, and our relationship and friendship grew to another level. Her faith in God began to increase as I shared more of God's truth with her through His Word.

In June 2015, she was blessed financially and felt God saying to her that she should sow part of this blessing into my life. She knew I like traveling and prayed about taking me on a trip. God then put everything in place for the trip to happen.

That year, for the weekend of my birthday, I received the gift of an all-expenses-paid trip to Miami with extra money for shopping. Thus far, that has been one of my best birthday gifts. I was thankful to God for His faithfulness in blessing me beyond my expectations. My friend said that I had been a blessing to her in intangible ways—more than I would ever know— and she was delighted to bless me in a tangible way. There was another side to this blessing that was sowed into my life. During a time of prayer, while we were on the trip, I told her I sensed that a promotion was on the way for her. About three days after her return to work, she messaged me with the great news of her promotion. GOD IS FAITHFUL!

Luke says it this way, "Give, and you will receive. Your gift will return to you in full—pressed down, shaken together to make room for more, running over, and poured into your lap.

The amount you give will determine the amount you get back"
(Luke 6:38).

I would like to end this chapter by sharing with you a powerful poem I came across some years ago that encapsulates what is written in this entire book. The title of the poem is "Wait" by Russell Kelfer (used by permission).

Wait

Desperately, helplessly, longingly, I cried.
Quietly, patiently, lovingly God replied.
I pled, and I wept for a clue to my fate,
And the Master so gently said, *Child you must wait!*

Wait? you say, *wait!* my indignant reply.
Lord, I need answers, I need to know why!
Is your hand shortened? Or have you not heard?
By *Faith* I have asked, and am claiming your Word.

My future, and all to which I can relate,
Hangs in the balance, and you tell me to *Wait?*
I'm needing a "yes," a go-ahead sign,
Or even a "no," to which I can resign.

And Lord, you promised that if we believe,
We need but to ask, and we shall receive.
And Lord, I've been asking, and this is my cry:
I'm weary of asking! I need a reply!

Then quietly, softly, I learned of my fate
As my Master replied once again, *You must wait.*
So, I slumped in my chair, defeated and taut

And grumbled to God, So, *I'm waiting … for what?*

He seemed then to kneel and His eyes wept with mine,
And he tenderly said, *I could give you a sign.*
I could shake the heavens, and darken the sun.
I could raise the dead, and cause mountains to run.
All you seek, I could give, and pleased you would be.
You would have what you want—but you wouldn't know Me.

You would not know the depth of my love for each saint;
You would not know the power that I give to the faint;
You would not learn to see through the clouds of despair;
You would not learn to trust just by knowing I am there;
You would not know the joy of resting in Me,
When darkness and silence were all you could see.

You would never experience that fullness of love
As the peace of My Spirit descends like a dove;
You would know that I give, and I save,
But you would not know the depth of the beat of my heart.

The glow of My comfort late into the night.
The faith that I give when you walk without sight,
The depth that is beyond getting just what you asked
Of an infinite God, who causes what you have to last.

You would never know, should your pain quickly flee,
What it means that My grace is sufficient for thee.
Yes, your dreams for your loved ones overnight would come true,
But oh, the loss!! If I lost what I am doing in you!

So be silent, my child, and in time you will see
That the greatest of gifts is to get to know me.

And though oft may my answers seem terribly late,
My wisest of answers is still, but to wait.

To find more poems and several hundred practical Bible messages by Russell Kelfer in both audio and print, visit www. dtm.org.

Personal Application

*For this is how God loved the world: He gave his
one and only Son, so that everyone who believes
in him will not perish but have eternal life.*

—John 3:16

*And this is the way to have eternal life—to know you, the
only true God, and Jesus Christ, the one you sent to earth.*

—John 17:3

You have now come to the end of my journey and have read
about my relationship with the Father through His Son. You
have also seen how I have grown in intimacy with the Father
through the Holy Spirit revealing His truths to me over the
years.

I would like to give you an opportunity to also have eternal life, which starts through a personal relationship with the Father.

Kindly say the following prayer genuinely from your heart as you ponder on the words:

> Our Father in heaven, may Your name be kept holy.
>
> I thank You for sharing with me through this book Your desire for me to know You more intimately through Your Son, Jesus.
>
> I acknowledge that I was conceived and born in sin.
>
> I am a sinner in need of a Savior.
>
> Thank You for providing Your one and only Son, Jesus Christ, to be this Savior for me.
>
> Jesus, please forgive me of all my sins.
>
> I now invite You into my life to become my Lord and Savior.
>
> Thank You for sending me the Holy Spirit to be my teacher and guide from this day onward in Jesus's name.
>
> Amen!

Congratulations! You are now a part of the family of God and should do the following:

1 - Obtain a Bible so that you can start your journey of knowing God through His Word.
2 - Find a Bible-believing church so that you can become a part of a local assembly in which you can be discipled.

You can also find out more about following Jesus in water baptism.

3 - Have a strong desire to grow in your relationship with God the Father, Jesus Christ the Son, and the Holy Spirit.

Enjoy your new journey of eternal life!

NOTES

Preface

    I.   John 17:3

Chapter 1: The Process

    I.   Definition of *process*—online dictionary, https://www.google.com/search?q=process

    II.   Galatians 5:22–23

    III.   Luke 22:42

    IV.   Ibid.

    V.   Hebrews 11:6 (KJV)

    VI.   John 10:27 (KJV)

    VII.   Psalm 139:1–10

    VIII. John 16:5–15

    IX.   Joshua 1:7–9

    X.   Proverbs 3:1–7

    XI.   John 14:15–21

    XII.   John 16:5–15

    XIII. 1 John 1:5–10

Chapter 2: Commencement of Missionary Journey
- I.   Mathew 14:28–29
- II.   Deuteronomy 19:15b
- III.   2 Corinthians 13:1b (KJV)

Chapter 3: First Mission aboard Logos Hope
- I.   Jeremiah 29:11
- II.   Psalm 121:7 (KJV)
- III.   Philippians 3:14 (KJV)
- IV.   2 Corinthians 1:4
- V.   John 17:3
- VI.   Jeremiah 18:14
- VII.   Isaiah 64:4
- VIII. 1 Corinthians 2:9
- IX.   Hebrews 11:29

Chapter 4: Second Mission aboard Logos Hope
- I.   Proverbs 19:21
- II.   Acts 20:31
- III.   Galatians 1:18
- IV.   Luke 22:42
- V.   Ibid.
- VI.   Percentage of Christianity in Japan, https://en.wikipedia.org/wiki/Religion_in_Japan
- VII.   Nick Vujicic, *Unstoppable*
- VIII. Psalm 23
- IX.   Isaiah 41:10
- X.   Mathew 20:20–26

Chapter 5: Third Mission aboard *Logos Hope*

I.   Jeremiah 33:3 (KJV)
II.   Psalm 37:23 (KJV)
III. Jeremiah 29:11
IV.   Psalm 121 (KJV)
V.   Jeremiah 1:5
VI.   Proverbs 18:16 (KJV)
VII. 2 Corinthians 12:12 (KJV)
VIII. Isaiah 46:9–10 (KJV)
IX.   Philippians 2:13
X.   2 Timothy 4:7 (KJV)
XI.   Isaiah 26:4 (KJV)
XII. Hebrews 6:19
XIII. Psalm 18:2 (KJV)
XIV. Jeremiah 29:13 (NKJV)

Chapter 6: God through the Generations

I.   Psalm 90:1–2
II.   Definition of Cocoa Panyols, https://en.wikipedia.org/wiki/Cocoa_panyols
III. Cape Coast Castle, https://en.wikipedia.org/wiki/Cape_Coast_Castle
IV.   Cape Verde, https://en.wikipedia.org/wiki/Cape_Verde
V.   Psalm 37:23
VI.   Mathew 1:2–17
VII. 2 Corinthians 5:18
VIII. Psalm 32:8
IX.   Philippians 1:6
X.   Romans 8:18
XI.   1 Peter 5:10
XII. Psalm 84:11

    XIII.   Jeremiah 29:11
    XIV.   Proverbs 3:5–6
    XV.   Isaiah 40:31
    XVI.   Isaiah 41:10
    XVII.   Psalm 46:10
    XVIII. Psalm 37:23

Chapter 7: *Waiting for My Husband—My Boaz*

    I.   Genesis 2:18
    II.   Lady in Waiting, Jackie Kendall and Debby Jones
    III.   Proverbs 4:23
    IV.   Definition of *heart*, https://dictionary.cambridge.org/dictionary/english/heart
    V.   Jeremiah 17:9 (KJV)
    VI.   2 Corinthians 5:17
    VII.   Numbers 23:19
    VIII.   Proverbs 18:22

Chapter 8: *Waiting through Transitions*

    I.   Ecclesiastes 3:1
    II.   Ecclesiastes 3:11
    III.   Psalm 18:34
    IV.   Galatians 5:16
    V.   Mathew 4:4
    VI.   Philippians 4:19
    VII.   Psalm 37:23
    VIII.   Isaiah 54:10 (NKJV)
    IX.   Philippians 4:7 (NKJV)
    X.   Ezekiel 33:7
    XI.   1 Samuel 30:6 (KJV)

XII. The Bamboo Tree Story, https://stunningmotivation.com/6-success-lessons-learn-bamboo-tree/

XIII. Pregnant for Years, https://www.babble.com/pregnancy/pregnant-for-years-20-animals-with-very-long-pregnancies-photos/

XIV. Burj Khalifa's Foundation Construction, https://www.sanyglobal.com/en_sa/cases/63.html

XV. Numbers 23:19

Chapter 9: Lessons Learned through Seasons of Waiting

I.   Isaiah 49:2 (KJV)
II.   Psalm 45:13 (KJV)
III.   Psalm 51:6 (NKJV)
IV.   Psalm 15:1–2 (NKJV)
V.   Colossians 3:23
VI.   Luke 6:44–45
VII.   Ephesians 6:18
VIII. Mathew 4:1–11 (NIV)
IX.   John 14:1–11
X.   1 Corinthians 4:1–2
XI.   Ezra 8:21–23

Chapter 10: The Importance of Sowing while Waiting

I.   Galatians 6:7–9
II.   Leviticus 27:30–32
III.   Hebrews 7:1–10
IV.   Luke 6:38
V.   "Wait" by Russel Kelfer, https://russellkelfer.org/poem-wait.htm

Appendix: Personal Application

I.   John 3:16
II.   John 17:3

ACKNOWLEDGMENTS

A great African proverb says, "It takes a village to raise a child." I do concur and can attest to this in my life. I would like to express my love and gratitude to everyone who contributed to my life, especially during my childhood. You all have helped shape me into the person I am today. Special thanks to my mother, Victoria Isidore; my grandmother, the late Mildred Isidore; all my aunts (Geraldine, Marcia, Joan, Heidi and Sherry Ann) and all my uncles (Elvis, Lawrence, Winston, Gregory and the late Carlton); and all my other extended family members.

To my earthly father, Martin Constantine, I missed having you in my life in the formative years, but I am thankful to Father God that we are now a part of each other's lives. I love and appreciate you! To your late wife, aunty Evelyn, I will always remember her as someone with a big heart as she embraced all your daughters as her own. I have fond memories of her, especially when she planned the special luncheon and invited all your children over to your home. To date, this was the only occasion in which your six children were under one roof.

I'm grateful to God for the foundation that He has given me at the Woodbrook Pentecostal Church, under the leadership of Rev. Osbert and Rev. Angela Williams, Rev. Joycelyn Nelson, and the late apostle Turnel Joshua Nelson. This foundation has contributed to the faith that I now possess. Thank you all for your dedication and commitment to the work of the Lord and for greatly impacting my life and journey. I'm also thankful to all the other men and women of God, who have contributed to my life and journey in one way or another.

To Sister Jacqueline Baird and the late apostle Bertril Baird, thank you for opening your home to disciple young men and women of God who needed that spiritual covering. This contribution to the kingdom of God has been priceless. Daddy Baird, you are dearly missed, and I can still hear your voice in my ear saying, "My daughter, how are you doing?" Your legacy will continue to live on in my life.

Heartfelt thanks to everyone who has sown into my life and ministry, especially when I ventured out into full-time missionary work. You have been a great team player in this partnership, and I know that God will continue to richly bless you.

A special mention must be given to three individuals: firstly, Rev. Emroy Sampson and his church for their unwavering support since I began this journey in 2010. I appreciate your love for the work of missions and for missionaries; secondly, Sister Esther—you have surprised me time and time again with your sacrificial giving, and for this, I say thank you; and thirdly, the late Ulric Anderson—you had the gift of giving, and your commitment toward my life and ministry has been admirable. I truly appreciated your efforts to stay in touch with me when I was on the field, especially for my birthday. I will forever remember your partnership.

Special thanks to all my covenant prayer partners for believing in me and standing with me over the years. Together, we were able to see the manifestation of some of my promises from God. Thank you to Theresa Andrews, Mary Beverly

Constantine, and Kim Joshua for being my sounding boards during the early stages of this book and also for being my initial proofreaders. I will forever be grateful for all your help. Love you all very much.

Thank you to the editor, publisher, graphic designer, and printer.

Love and thanks to all my friends who have become like family. You have loved me, supported me, encouraged me, and prayed for me along the way. I am a better person for having you in my life and as part of my journey. A special mention is made of Juliet and her family and to my childhood best friend, Tricia Pierre, whom I have known since I was five years old.

Thank you to my darling husband, "Prince" Patrick Murray Musgrave, for all your hard work and patience as we went through the final manuscript before it was sent to the publisher. I love you plenty, plenty, plenty!

Finally, thank you to my Daddy God, my Lord and Savior and soon-coming King Jesus Christ, and my best friend, the Holy Spirit. Without You on my team, I would not have been able to write this book, nor would I have been able to make it thus far on this journey. Thank You for creating me in Your image and likeness and for giving my life meaning and purpose.

ABOUT THE AUTHOR

Susan Isidore, now Musgrave, is from a quaint little village in the northern part of the island of Trinidad and comes from a Roman Catholic background. In her teenage years, she was exposed to the gospel of Jesus Christ at the Woodbrook Pentecostal Church. During early adulthood, she committed her life to following Jesus. However, she did not fully surrender her entire heart until 1998 when God called her into a deeper relationship with Himself.

Susan has been fully committed to the Lord for over twenty-four years. She began her missionary journey in 2005 when she visited Venezuela. After this, she did mission work on the island of Grenada and the southern part of Trinidad. She then launched into full-time missionary work in 2010. During this time, she visited a number of countries in North Africa, the Arabian Peninsula, Asia, West, and South Africa, the Caribbean region, and Latin America.

Susan is an excellent communicator of the Word of God and imparts concise knowledge through her gift of teaching. She has a great love for God and people and is passionate about the Word of God. Susan's greatest desire is to empower others through teaching, training, and mentoring. Part of her mission is to encourage others to fulfill their God-given purpose.

Susan graduated from the West Indies School of Theology with a bachelor's degree in Bible and theology. She has gained extensive knowledge in financial and management accounting level 1 BSc from the Association of Certified Chartered Accountants. She has worked in the private sector at a professional level in the areas of administration, accounting, and finance.

Susan and her husband, Patrick Musgrave, are involved in full-time ministry and currently reside in Trinidad and Tobago. They can be viewed on their Facebook ministry called "Word in Focus."

Author's Email Address: author2019si@gmail.com